Usually, a guide for kalimba offers the possibility of playing by letter or by number, with letters being more common. The modern kalimba often has engraved letters representing the name of the notes. Under the engraved letter (or above the number), you can find one or two dots. These dots represent the octave above the center octave. We also put dots under the letters in the sheet music if they use an octave other than the main kalimba octave.

In this book, we recommend playing by letter and/or color.
Even if the signs are not engraved on the keys, normally, however, each kalimba has letter-coded stickers included in the set. Usually, they are not color-coded and since our book doesn't include stickers, we suggest making color-coded stickers yourself. This is very easy and you can do it with very small pieces of colored paper.

The color of the notes on your keys must be the same as the colors above.

Our sheet music is not for a specific kalimba but is universal and suitable for 8-17 note kalimbas.

The low notes are in the center of the kalimba. The notes become higher as you move away from the center. The order of the notes alternates from right to left, going outward as you move up the scale. Taking "C D E F G A B C", "C" is on the right side, and then you will find "D" on the left.

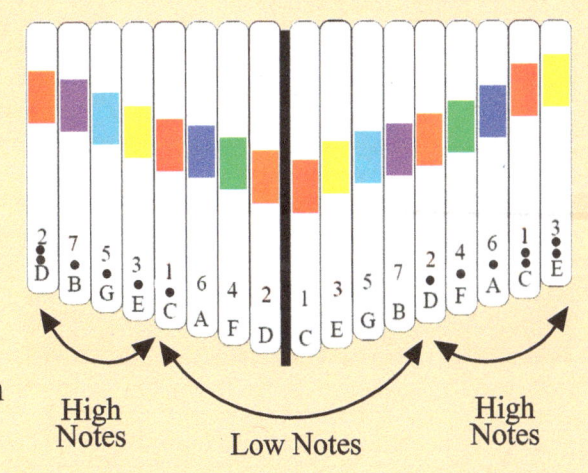

We made our pictured sheet music as simple as possible, songs have been transposed for a diatonic range. Some melodies might be changed and simplified. You'll quickly begin to play by letter-coded circles.

Part 1
Folk Songs

PART 1. Folk Songs 1

Au Clair de la Lune 2
Aura Lee 3
Barbara Allen 4
Billy Boy 5
Billy the Kid 6
Boil Them Cabbage Down 8
Buckeye Jim 9
Buffalo Gals 11
Colorado Trail 12
Cotton Eyed Joe 13
East Virginia Blues 14
Good Night Ladies 15
House of the Rising Sun 16
Jolly Good Fellow 17
Lavender's Blue 18
Li'l Liza Jane 19
Midnight on the Stormy Deep 20
My Bonnie 22
New River Train 23
Ninety Nine Bottles 24
Oh! Susannah 26
On Top of Old Smokey 27
Peace Like a River 28
Shenandoah 29

PART 2. Gospel Songs 30

Au Clair de la Lune

F F F G A G F A G G F
By the light of the moon, My friend Pier - rot,

F F F G A G F A G G F
Please lend me your quill pen. Just to write a word.

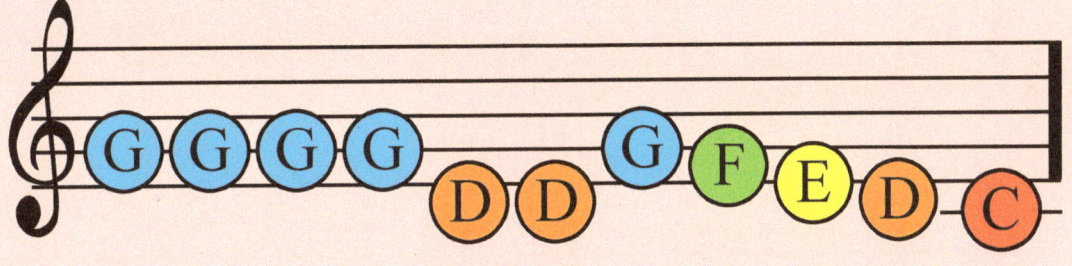

G G G G D D G F E D C
My candle is dead now and I have no light left.

F F F G A G F A G G F
O - pen your door for me. For the love of God.

Aura Lee

C F E F G D G F E D E
As the black-bird in the spring, "Neath the wil-low

F C C F E F G D G
tree,___ Sat and piped, I heard him sing,

F E D E F A A A A A A
Sing-ing Au - ra Lee. Au - ra Lee, Au - ra Lee,

A G F G A A A B A
Maid of gold- en hair, Sun - shine came a-

G D G F F E A G F
long with thee, And swal-lows in the air.

Barbara Allen

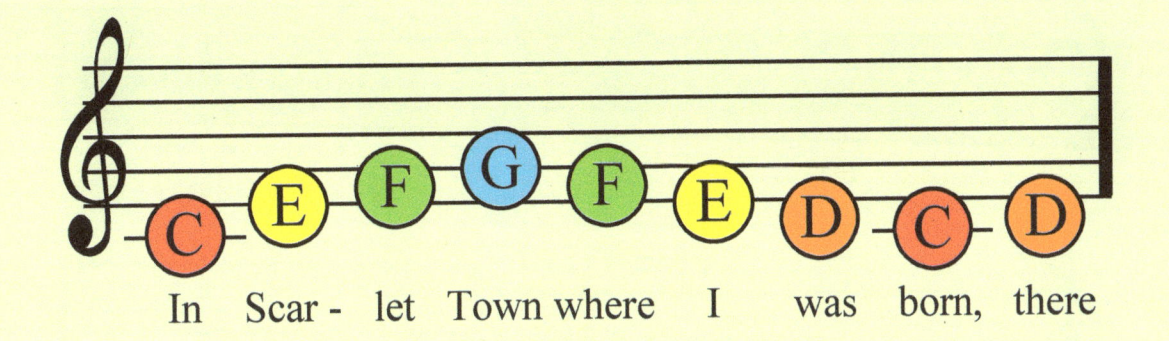

C E F G F E D C D
In Scar - let Town where I was born, there

E G C C B G B C A F A
was a fair maid dwel - lin'. Made ev' - ry youth cry,

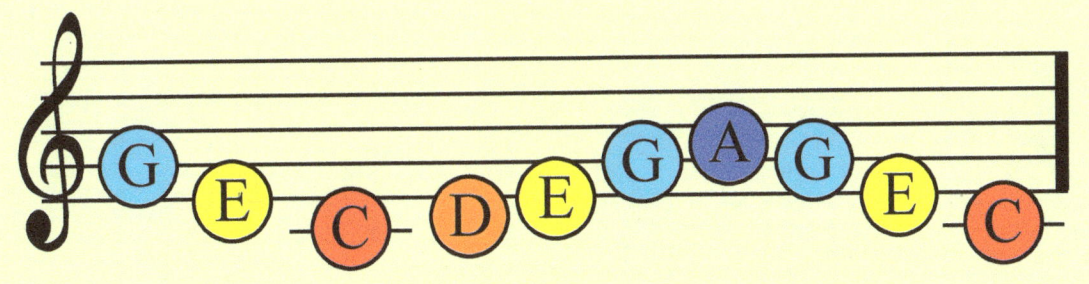

G E C D E G A G E C
well - a - day! Her name was Bar - b'ra Al - len.

Billy Boy

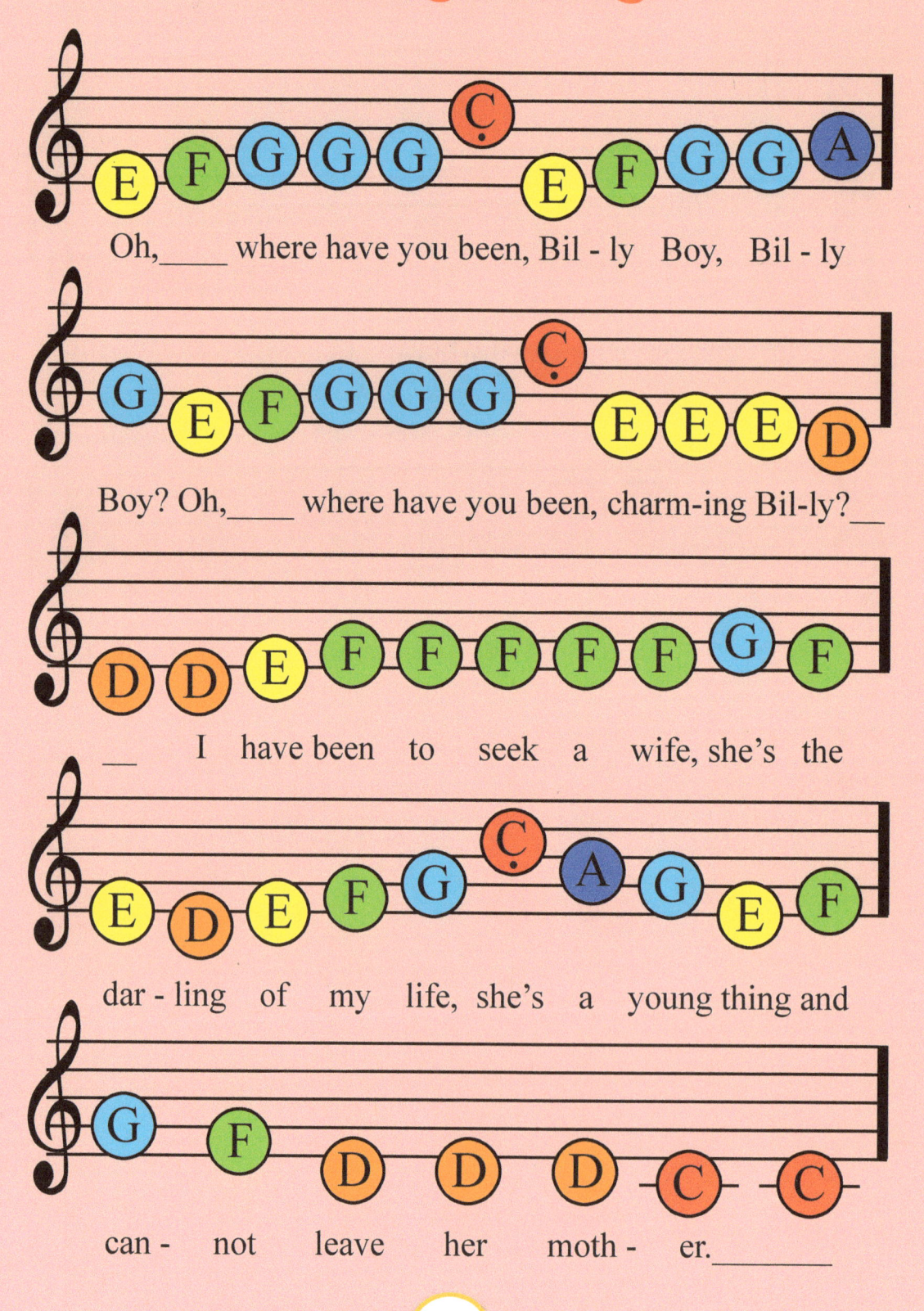

E F G G G C E F G G A
Oh, where have you been, Bil - ly Boy, Bil - ly

G E F G G G C E E E D
Boy? Oh, where have you been, charm-ing Bil-ly?

D D E F F F F F F G F
I have been to seek a wife, she's the

E D E F G C A G E F
dar - ling of my life, she's a young thing and

G F D D D C C
can - not leave her moth - er.

Billy the Kid

G G G G E E E F E F D
I'll sing you a true song of Bil- ly the Kid,

G G G E E E F E F D D
sing of the des- per- ate deeds that he did. Way

C C C E D C F F G
out in New Mex- i- co long, long a-

A A A G G G G G G
go, when a man's on- ly friend was his

G D E C
own for- ty- four.

Boil Them Cabbage Down

E E E E F F E E G E

Boil them cab - bage down, down. Turn them hoe cakes

D D E E E C F F F G

round. The on - ly song that I can sing is

E E E D C G G G E

boil them cab - bage down. Went up on a

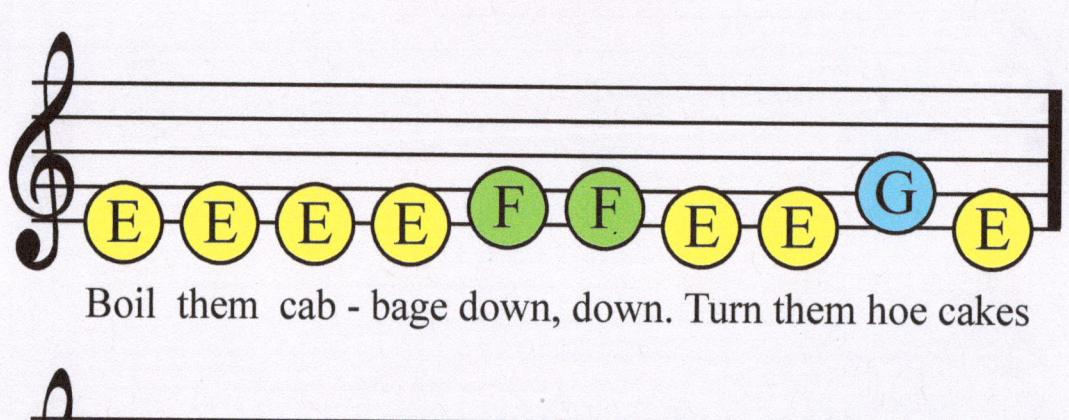

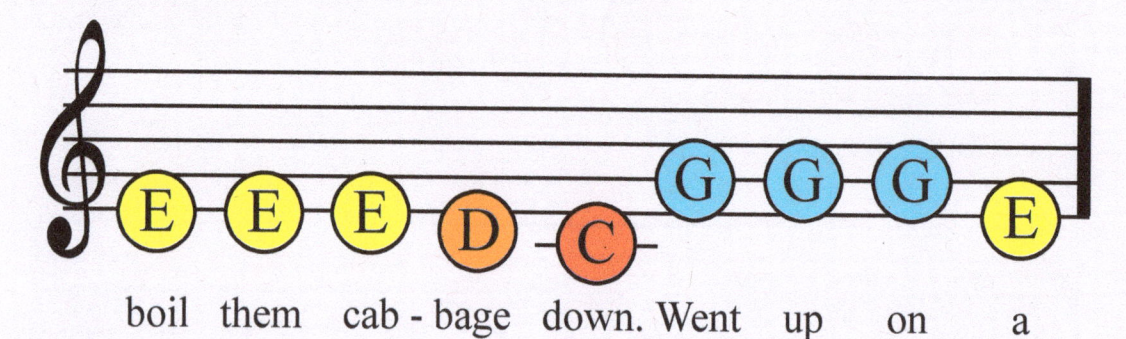

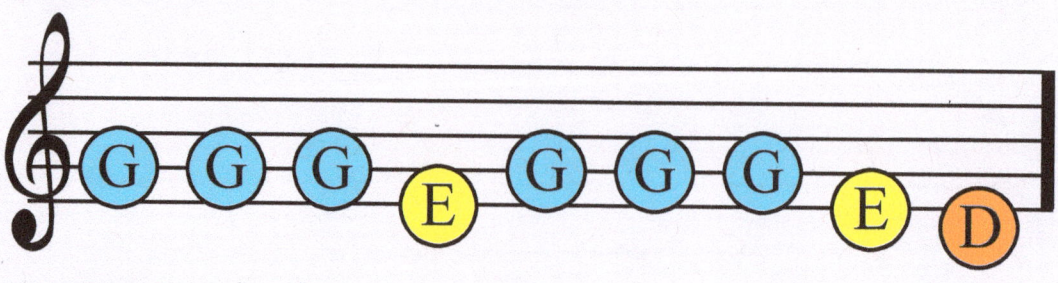

G G G E G G G E D

moun - tain, just to give my horn a blow.

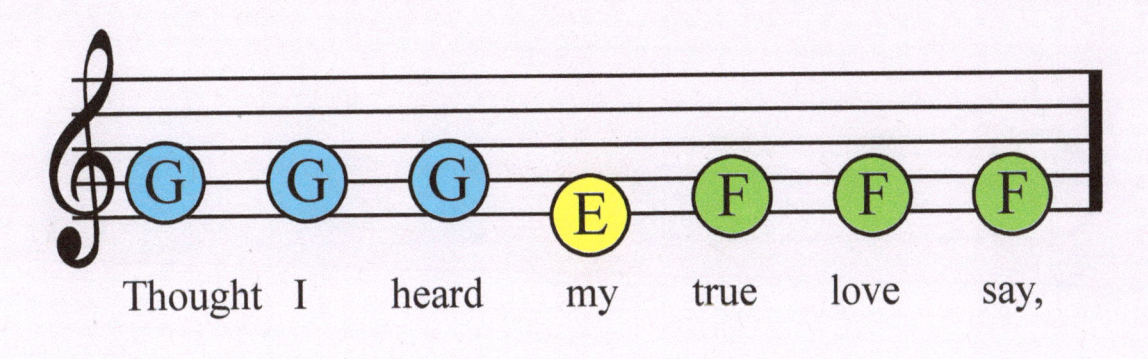

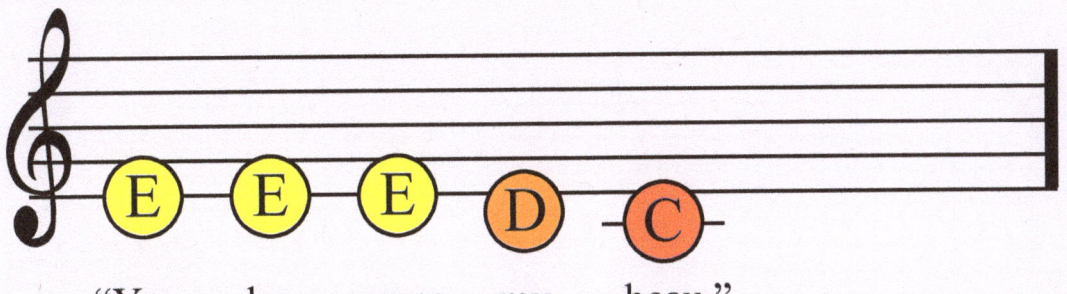

G G G E F F F

Thought I heard my true love say,

E E E D C

"Yon - der comes my beau."

Buckeye Jim

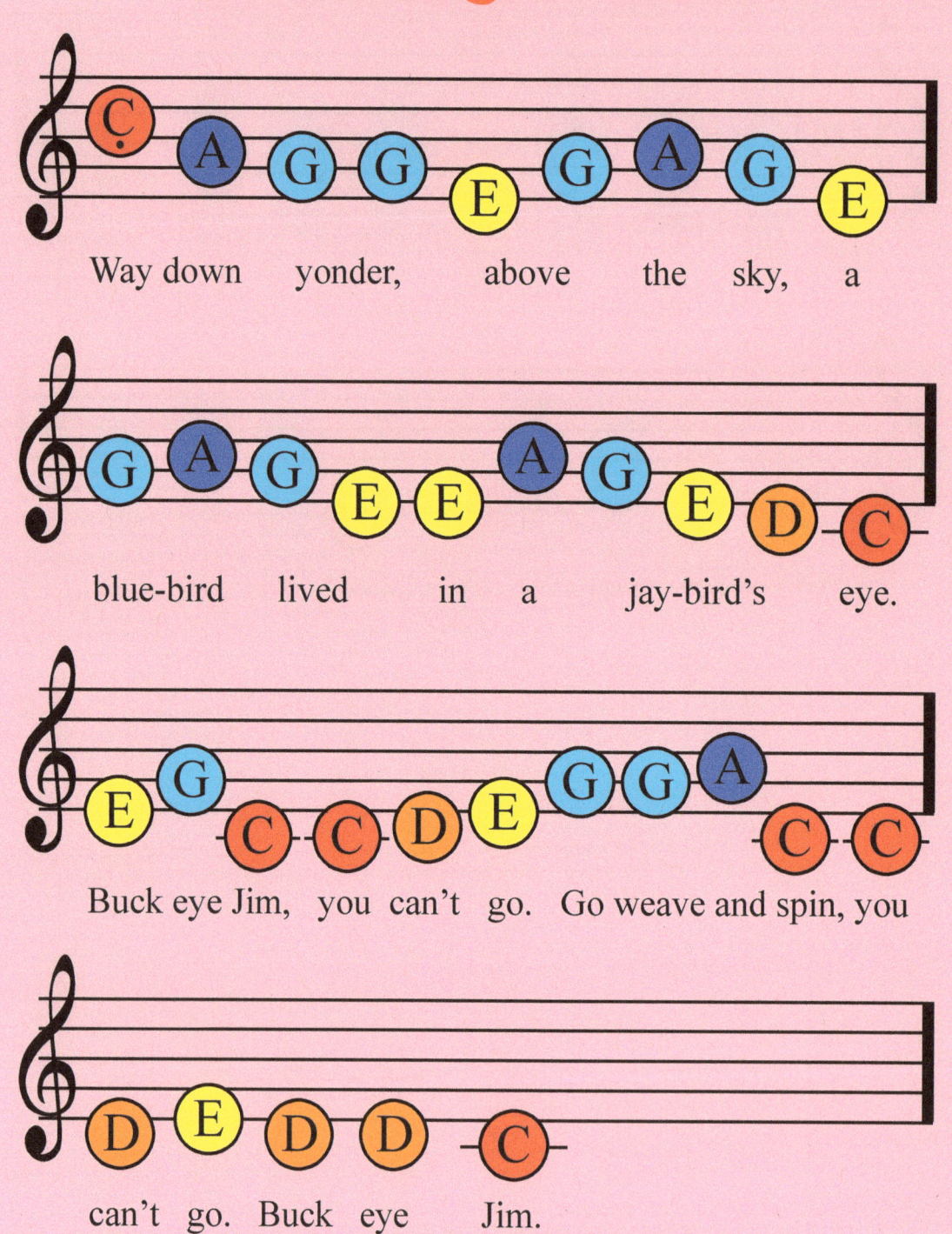

Way down yonder, above the sky, a blue-bird lived in a jay-bird's eye.

Buck eye Jim, you can't go. Go weave and spin, you can't go. Buck eye Jim.

Buffalo Galls

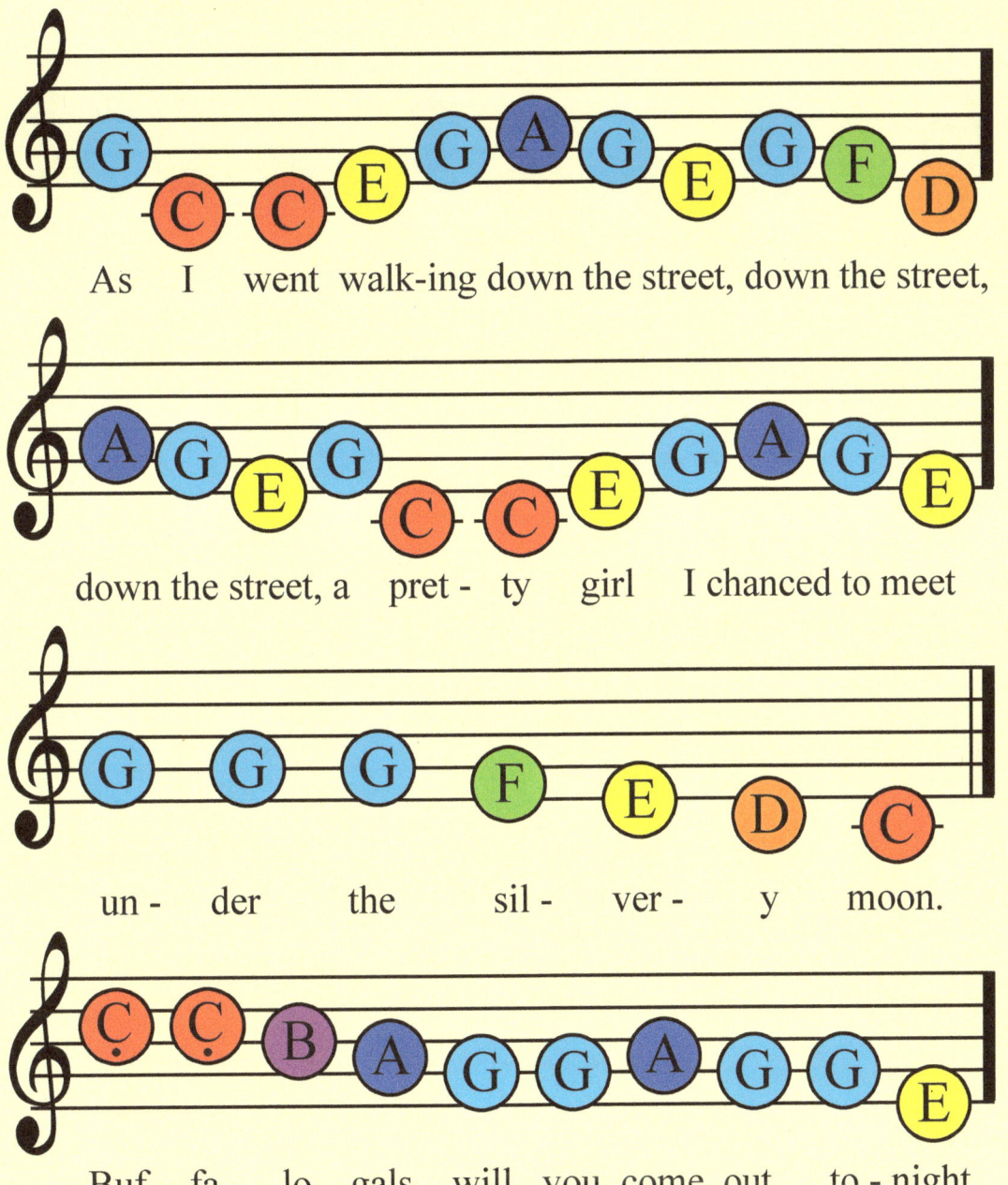

As I went walk-ing down the street, down the street,

down the street, a pret - ty girl I chanced to meet

un - der the sil - ver - y moon.

Buf - fa - lo gals, will you come out to - night,

come out to - night, come out to - night,

Buf - fa - lo gals, will you come out to-night, and

dance by the light of the moon.

Colorado Trail

E G G A G E D C D E
Eyes like a morn-ing star, cheeks like a rose,

E G G A G E E
Lau - ra was a pret - ty girl

C C D C D E G G A G E
God Al-might-y knows! Weep all you lit-tle rains,

D C D E G A C A
wail, winds, ___ wail, all a - long, a -

G E D C D C C C C
long, a - long the Col - o - rad - o trail.

12

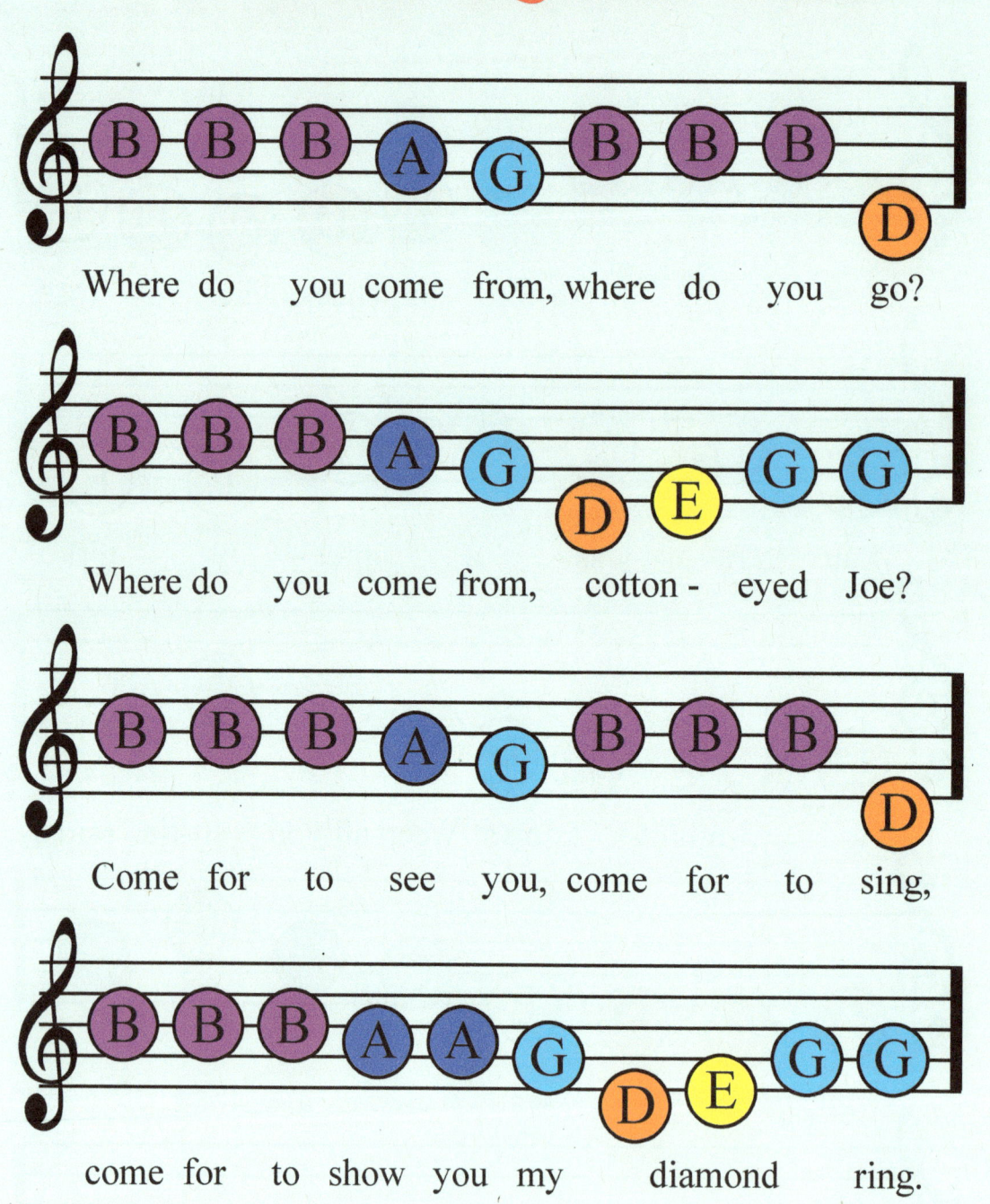

Cotton Eyed Joe

B B B A G B B B D

Where do you come from, where do you go?

B B B A G D E G G

Where do you come from, cotton - eyed Joe?

B B B A G B B B D

Come for to see you, come for to sing,

B B B A A G D E G G

come for to show you my diamond ring.

East Virginia Blues

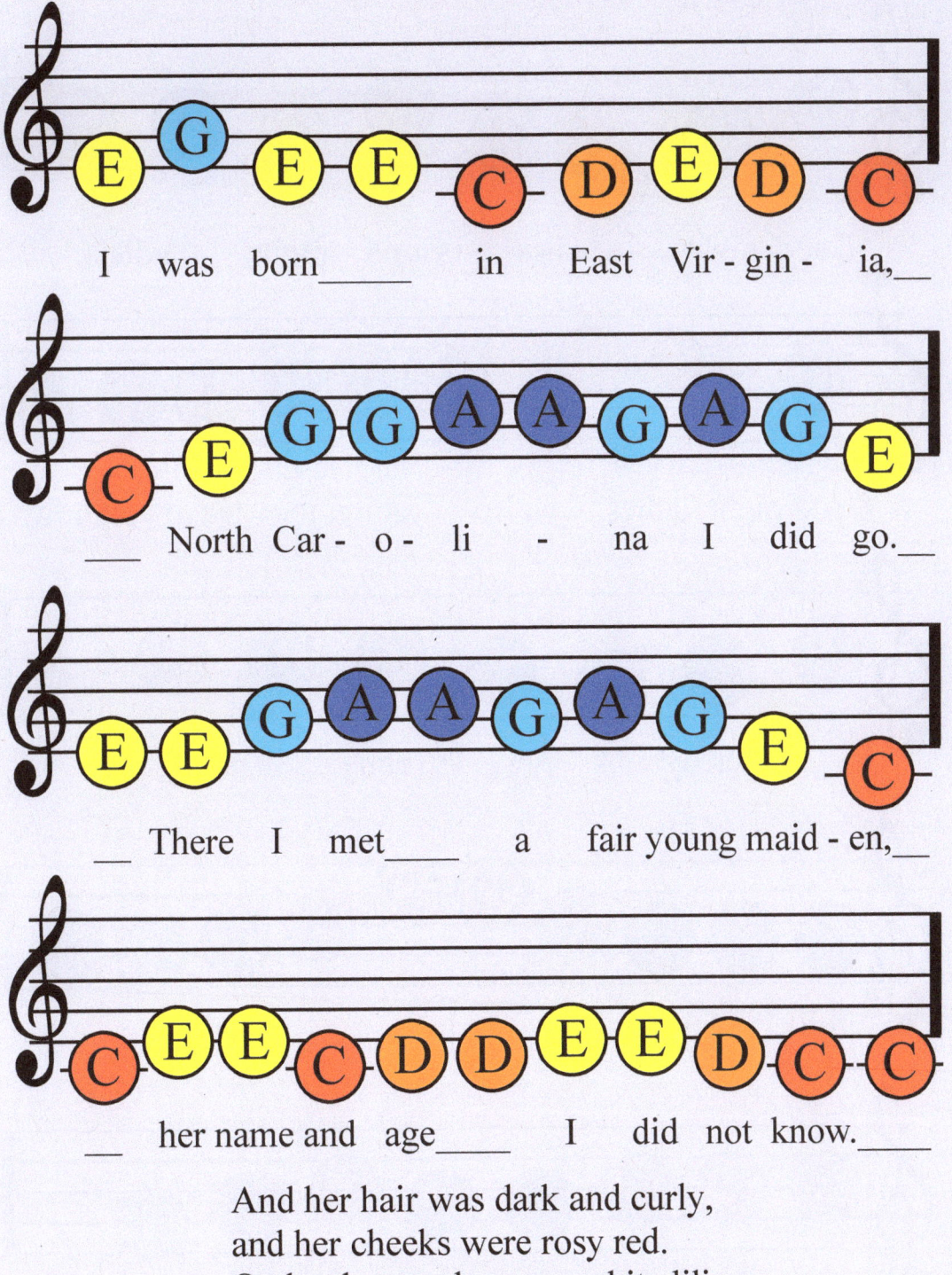

E G E E C D E D C
I was born___ in East Vir- gin- ia,___

C E G G A A G A G E
___ North Car- o- li- na I did go.___

E E G A A G A G E C
___ There I met___ a fair young maid- en,___

C E E C D D E E D C C
___ her name and age___ I did not know.___

And her hair was dark and curly,
and her cheeks were rosy red.
On her breast she wore white lilies
and there I longed to lay my had.

Good Night Ladies

B G D G B G A A
Good night, ladies! Good night, ladies!

B G C C C B B B A A G
Good night, ladies, we're going to leave you now.

B A G A B B B
Merrily we roll along,

A A A B D D B A G A
roll along, roll along, merrily we

B B B A A B A G
roll along, o'er the dark blue sea.

15

House of the Rising Sun

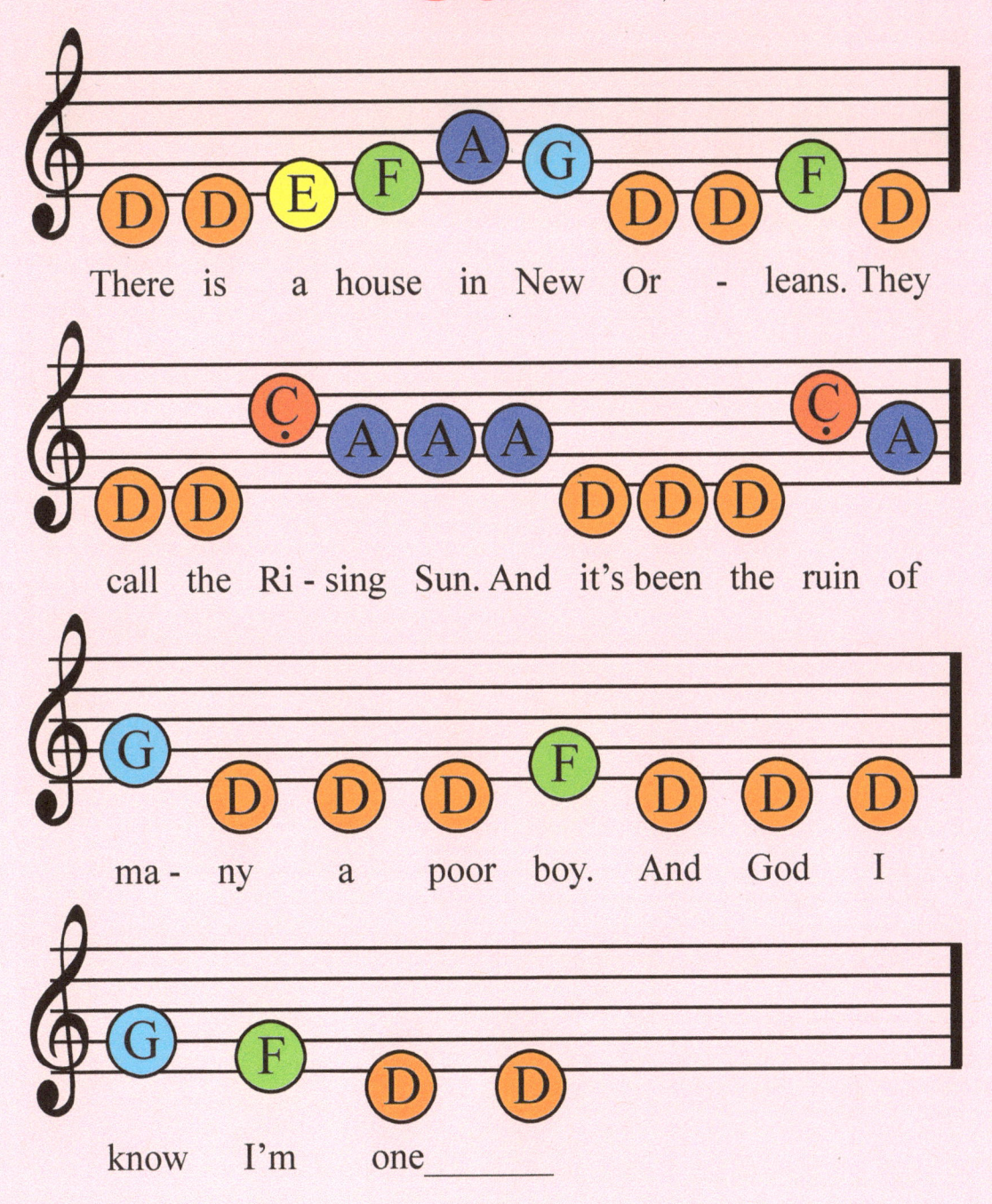

D D E F A G D D F D

There is a house in New Or - leans. They

D D C A A A D D D C A

call the Ri - sing Sun. And it's been the ruin of

G D D D F D D D

ma - ny a poor boy. And God I

G F D D

know I'm one

Jolly Good Fellow

C E E E D E F E E
For he's a jol - ly good fel - low, for

D D D C D E C C
he's a jol - ly good fel - low, for

E E E D E F A A
he's a jol - ly good fel - low, which

G G G F D C C
no - bo - dy can de - ny!

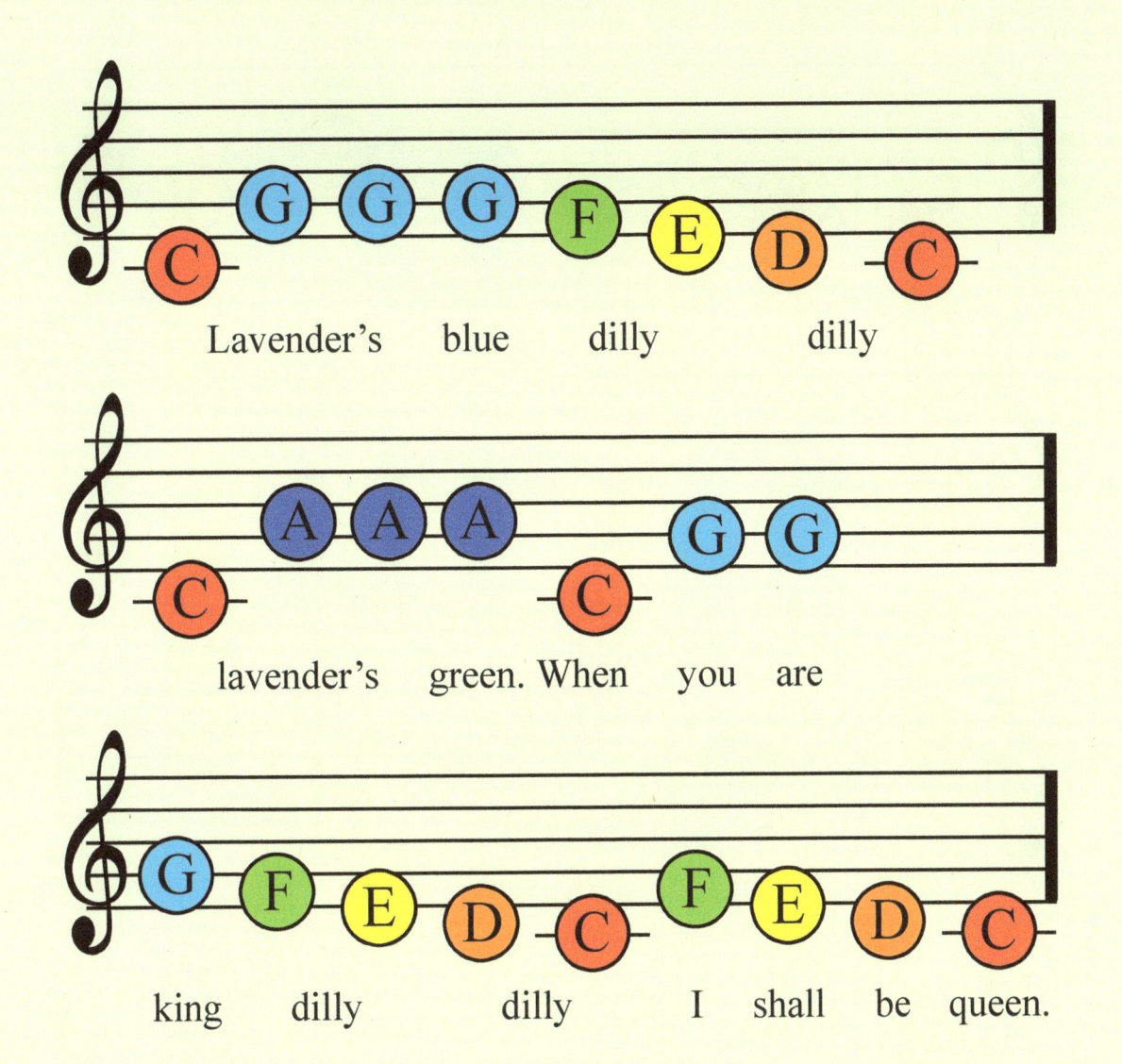

Lavender's Blue

C G G G F E D C
Lavender's blue dilly dilly

C A A A C G G
lavender's green. When you are

G F E D C F E D C
king dilly dilly I shall be queen.

Li'l Liza Jane

E E E D C E G G A G E G

I've got a house in Bal-ti-more, Li'l Li-za Jane.

E E D C E G G E E D C

Street car runs right by my door. Li'l Li-za Jane.

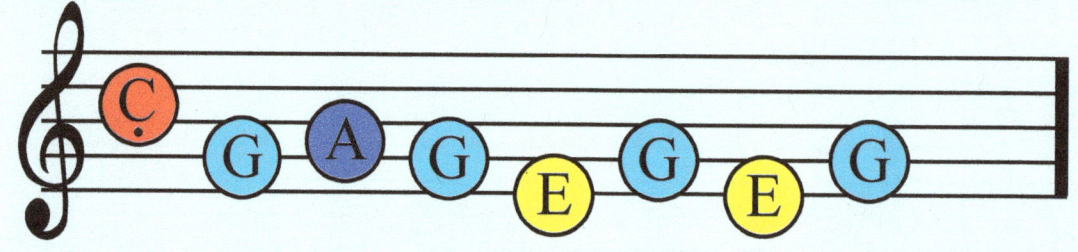

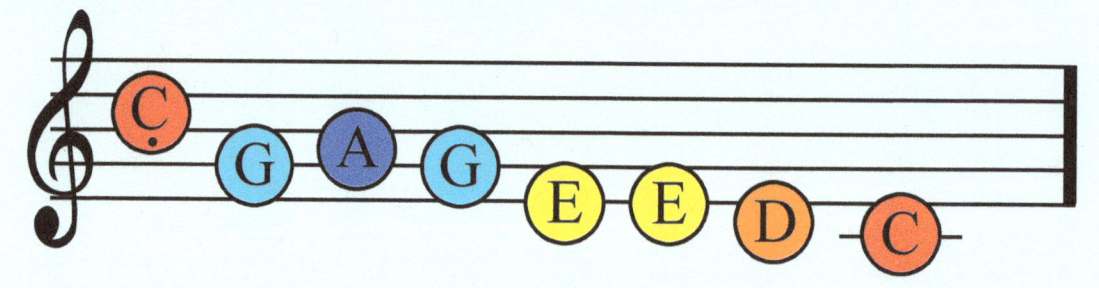

C G A G E G E G

Oh, E-li-za, Li'l Li-za Jane.

C G A G E E D C

Oh, E-li-za, Li'l Li-za Jane.

Midnight on the Stormy Deep

C E G E C D D C
T'was mid - night on the storm - y deep,

D E F G G G A G E
my so - li - ta - ry watch I'd keep.

E C C C C C A F A G
And I think of her I'd left be - hind,

G A E G C D D C
and asked if she'd be true and kind.

My Bonnie

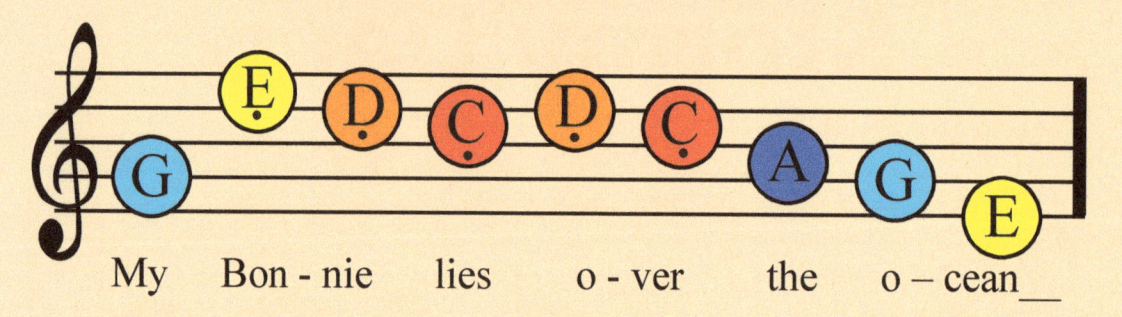

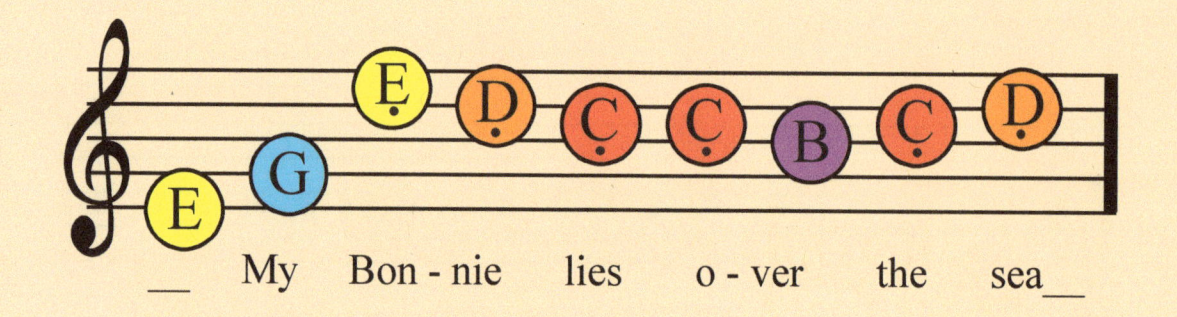

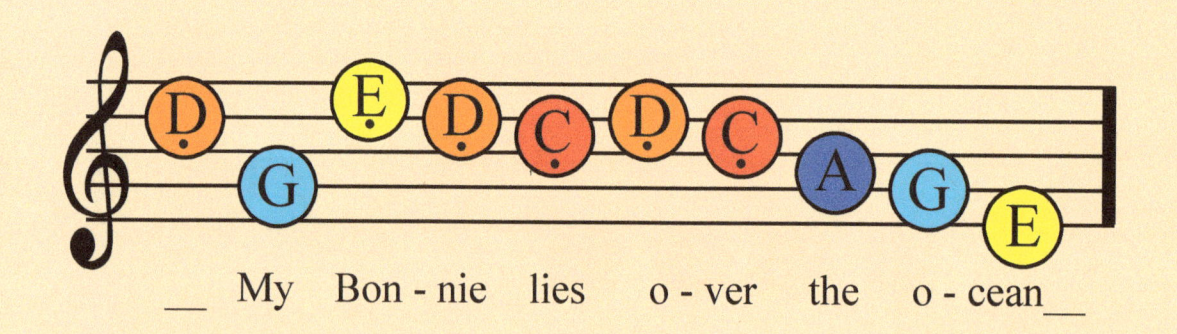

My Bon - nie lies o - ver the o - cean

My Bon - nie lies o - ver the sea

My Bon - nie lies o - ver the o - cean

Oh, bring back my Bon - nie to me

Bring back, bring back. Bring back my Bon - nie to me, to

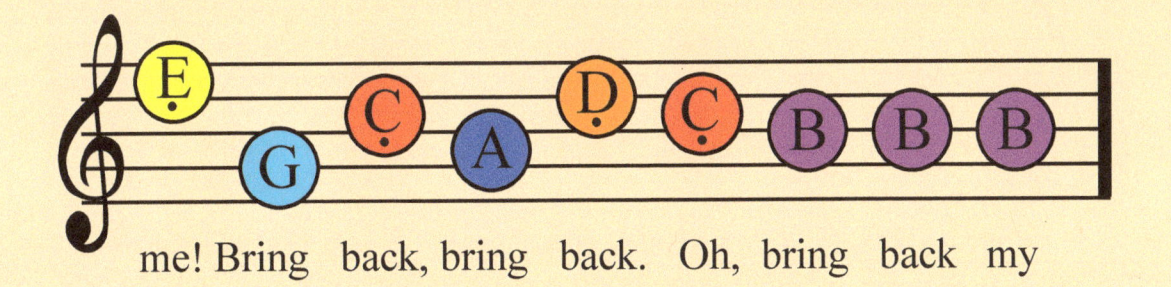

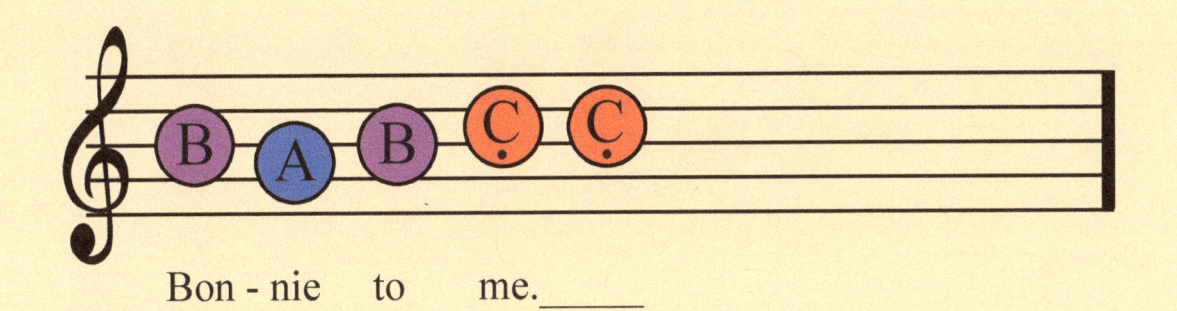

me! Bring back, bring back. Oh, bring back my

Bon - nie to me._____

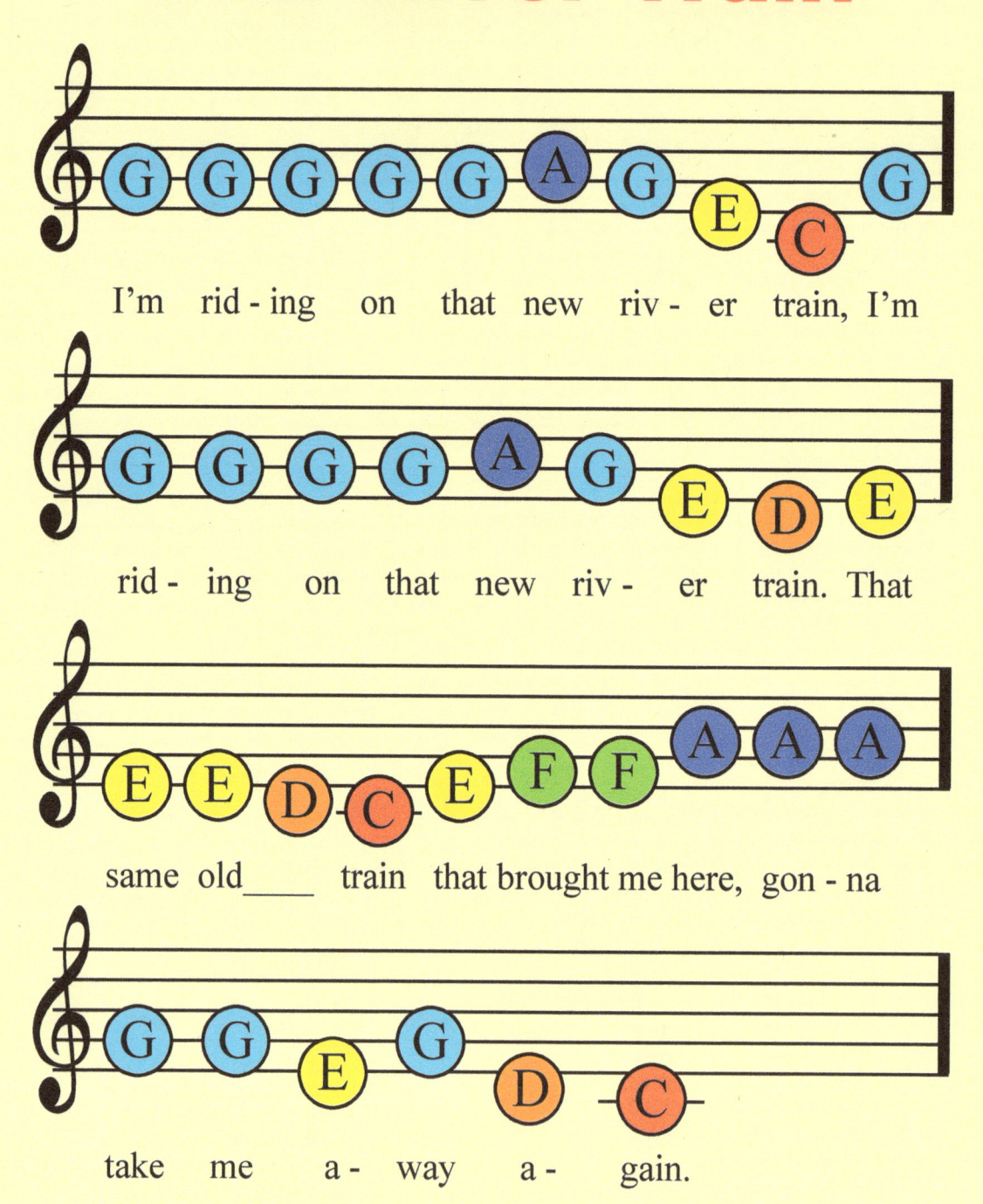

New River Train

I'm rid - ing on that new riv - er train, I'm
(G G G G G A G E C G)

rid - ing on that new riv - er train. That
(G G G G A G E D E)

same old___ train that brought me here, gon - na
(E E D C E F F A A A)

take me a - way a - gain.
(G G E G D C)

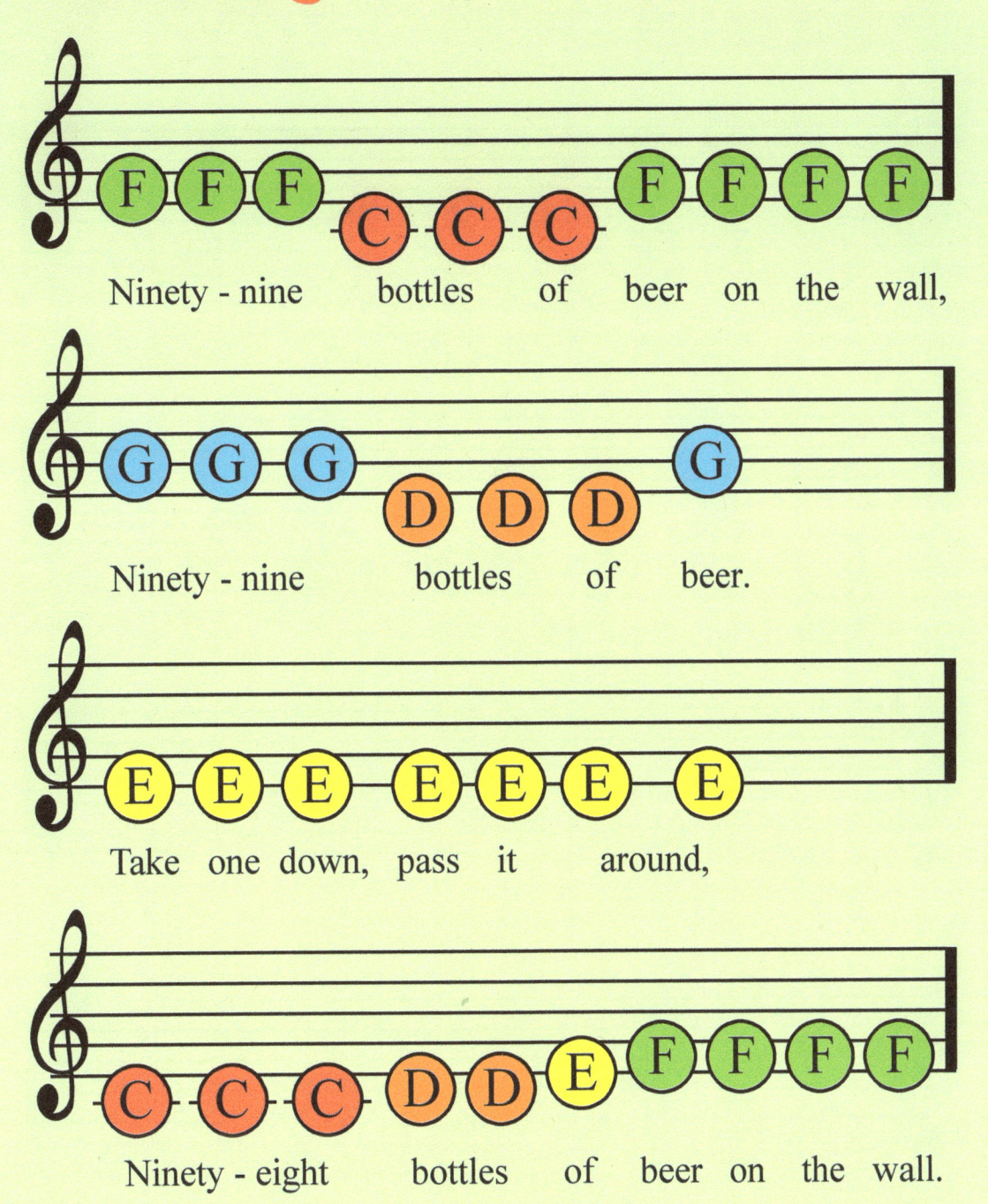

Ninety Nine Bottles

F F F C C C F F F F
Ninety - nine bottles of beer on the wall,

G G G D D D G
Ninety - nine bottles of beer.

E E E E E E E
Take one down, pass it around,

C C C D D E F F F F
Ninety - eight bottles of beer on the wall.

Oh! Susannah

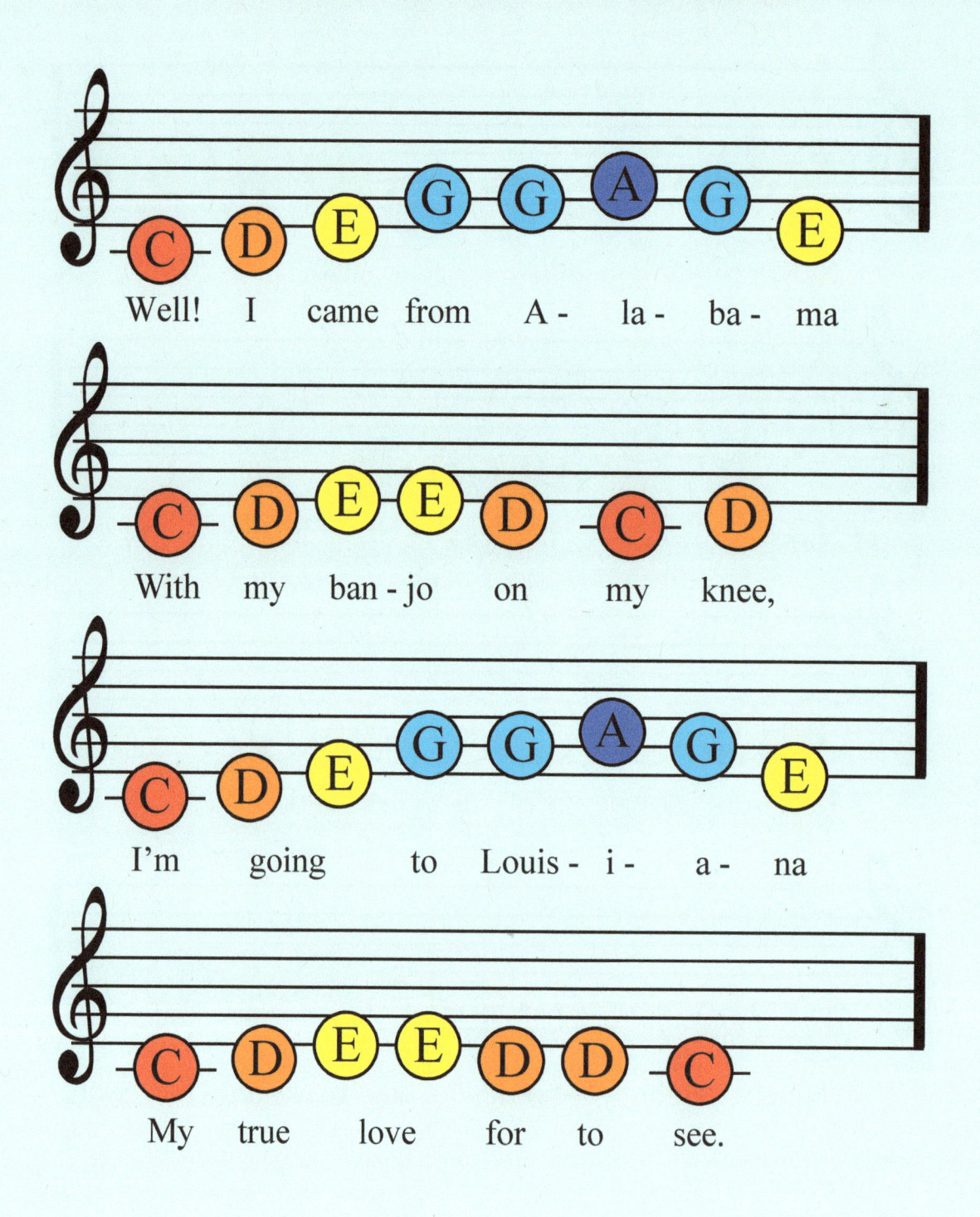

Well! I came from A- la- ba- ma
(C D E G G A G E)

With my ban- jo on my knee,
(C D E E D C D)

I'm going to Louis- i- a- na
(C D E G G A G E)

My true love for to see.
(C D E E D D C)

Oh! Su - san - nah, Don't you cry for me

I come from A - la - ba - ma

With my ban - jo on my knee.

On Top of Old Smokey

On top of old Smo - key,
(C C E G C A)

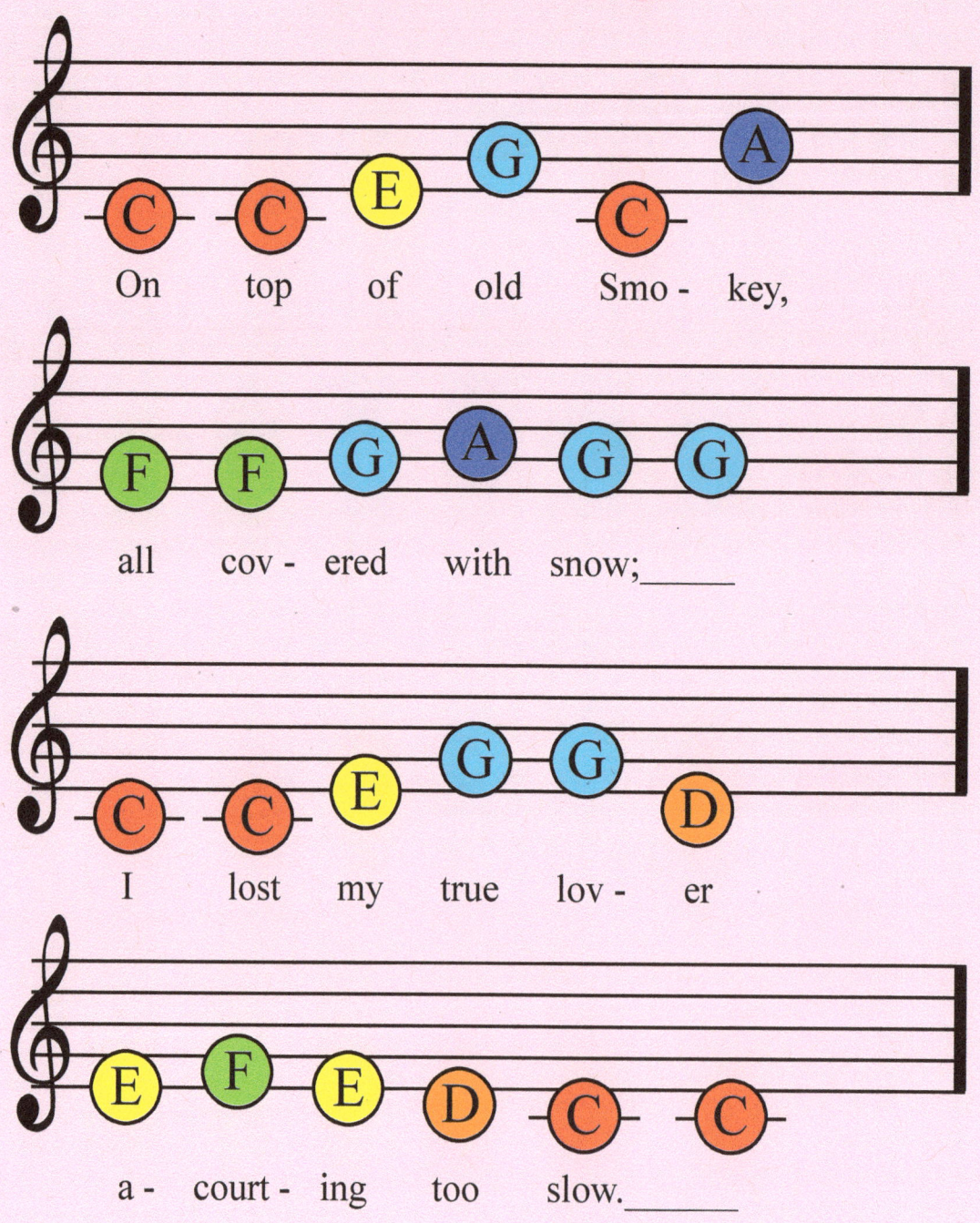

all cov - ered with snow;
(F F G A G G)

I lost my true lov - er
(C C E G G D)

a - court - ing too slow.
(E F E D C C)

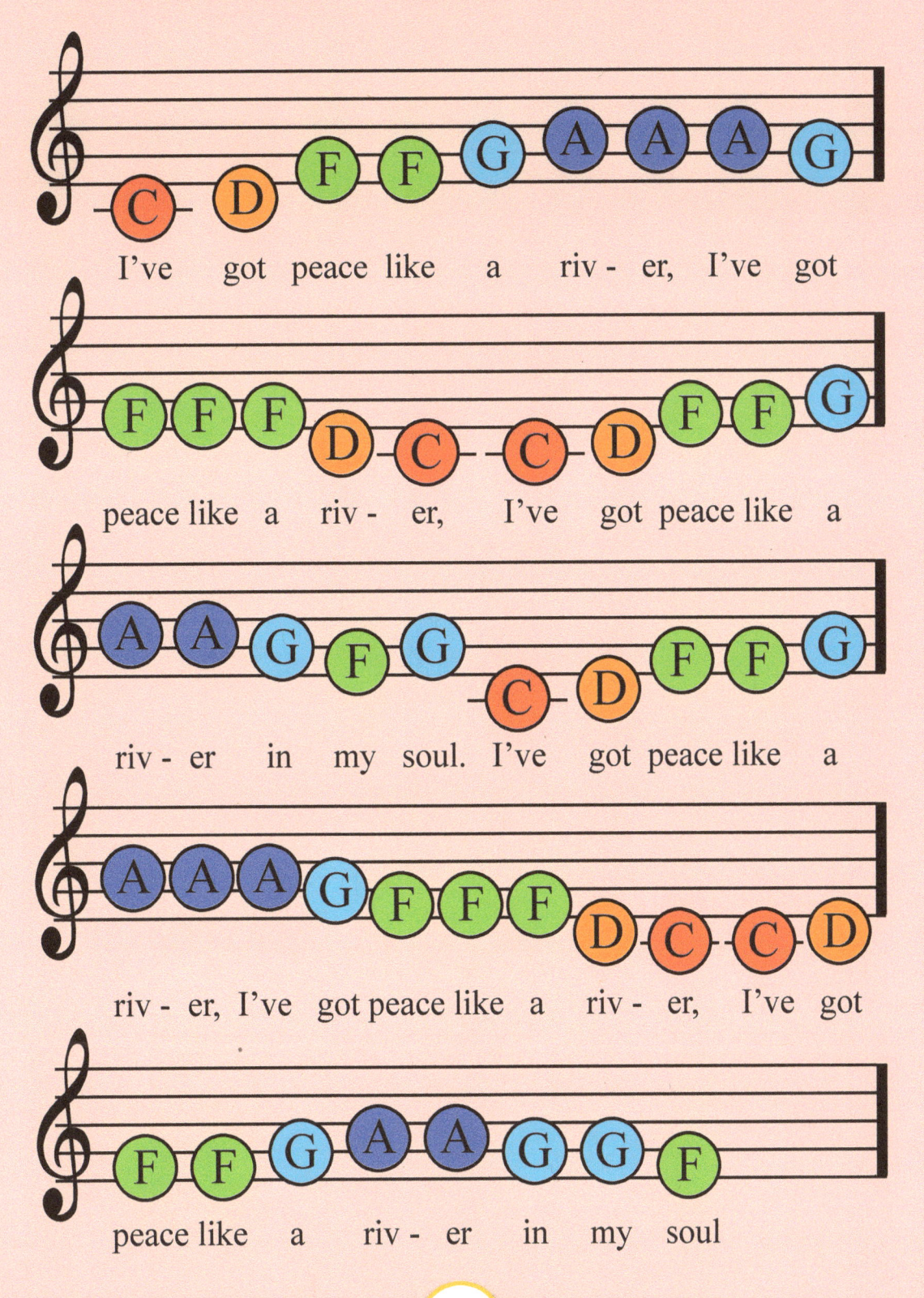

Peace like a River

C D F F G A A A G
I've got peace like a riv - er, I've got

F F F D C C D F F G
peace like a riv - er, I've got peace like a

A A G F G C D F F G
riv - er in my soul. I've got peace like a

A A A G F F F D C C D
riv - er, I've got peace like a riv - er, I've got

F F G A A G G F
peace like a riv - er in my soul

Shenandoah

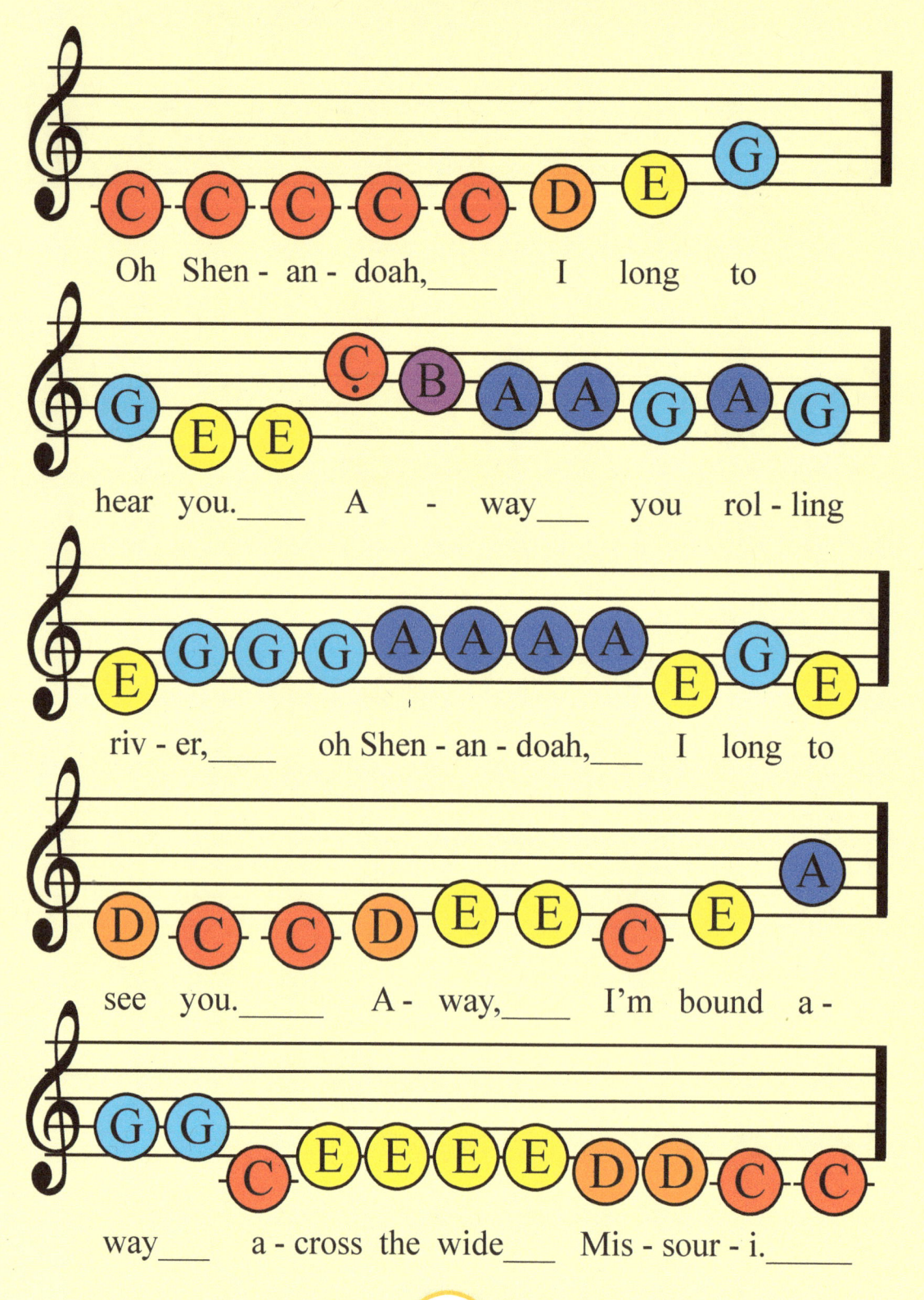

C C C C C D E G
Oh Shen - an - doah,___ I long to

G E E C B A A G A G
hear you.___ A - way___ you rol - ling

E G G G A A A A E G E
riv - er,___ oh Shen - an - doah,___ I long to

D C C D E E C E A
see you.___ A - way,___ I'm bound a -

G G C E E E E D D C C
way___ a - cross the wide___ Mis - sour - i.___

29

Part 2
Gospel Songs

Amazing Grace 31
Babylon's Falling 32
Christ Was Born on Christmas Day 33
Elijah Rock 34
Every Time I Feel the Spirit 35
Go, Tell It on the Mountain 36
God Is So Good 38
Great Big Stars 39
Great Day 40
He's God the Whole World in His Hands 42
Holy, Holy, Holy 44
I've Got Joy Joy 46
I've Got Peace Like a River 48
Jesus Loves Me 49
Jesus Walked This Lonesome Valley 51
Joy to the World! The Lord Is Come! 52
Just As I Am 54
Kumbaya, My Lord 55
Michael Row the Boat Ashore 56
Nobody Knows the Trouble I've Seen 57
Praise Him, All You Little Children 59
Shall We Gather at the River 60
Silent Night, Holy Night 62
Sinner Man 64
Soldier of the Cross 65
Somebody's Knockin' at Your Door 66
Song of Praise 68
Swing Love, Sweet Chariot 69
The Little Light of Mine... 71
There's a Meeting Here Tonight 73
We Are Climbing Jacob's Ladder 75
We Are Marching (Siyahamba) 76
We Shall Overcome 79
When the Saints Go Marching In 80
Who Built the Ark? 81
Will the Circle Be Unbroken 83

Amazing Grace

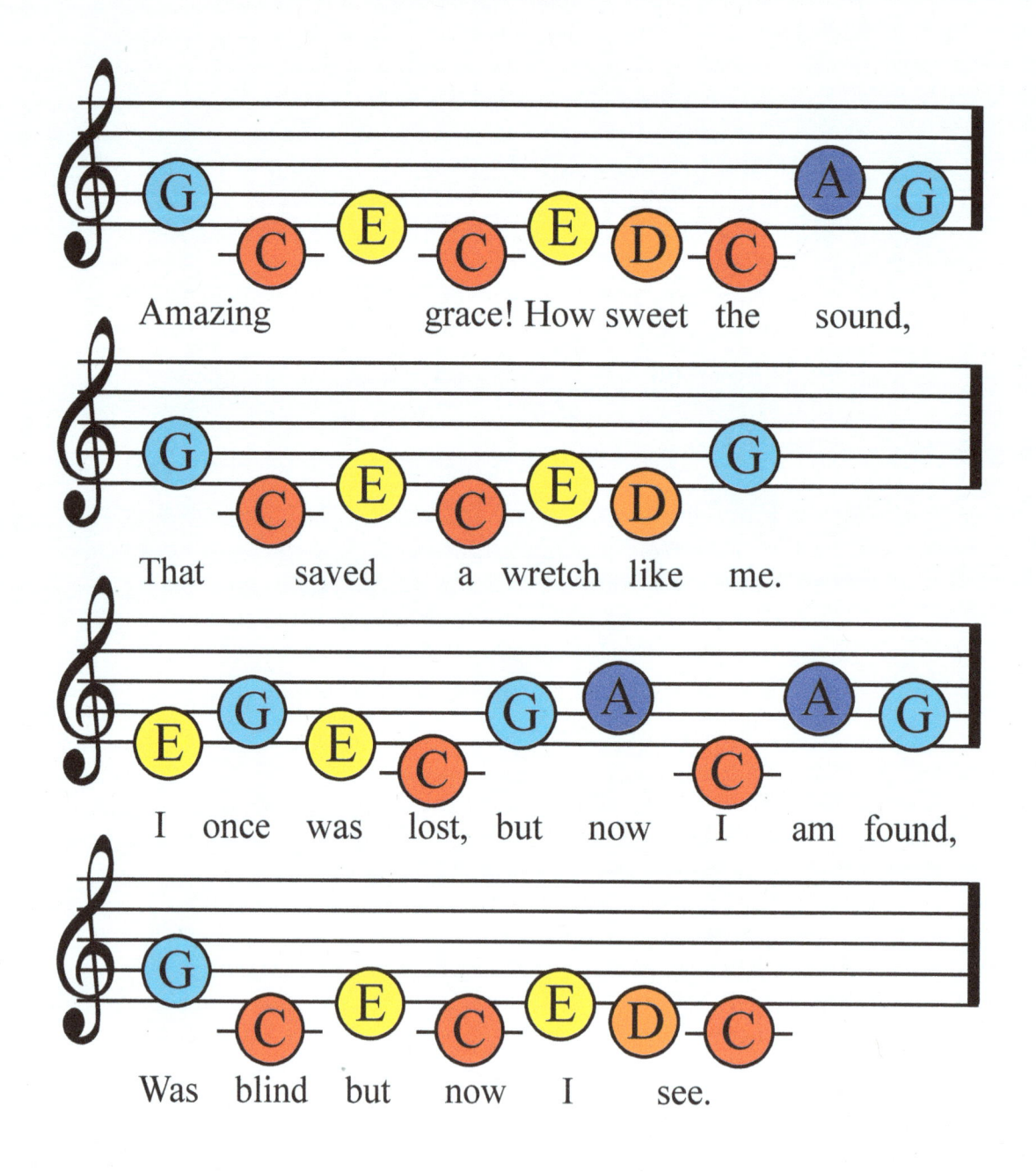

G C E C E D C A G
Amazing grace! How sweet the sound,

G C E C E D G
That saved a wretch like me.

E G E C G A C A G
I once was lost, but now I am found,

G C E C E D C
Was blind but now I see.

Was Grace that taught my heart to fear
And Grace, my fears relieved
How precious did that Grace appear
The hour I first believed

Babylon's Falling

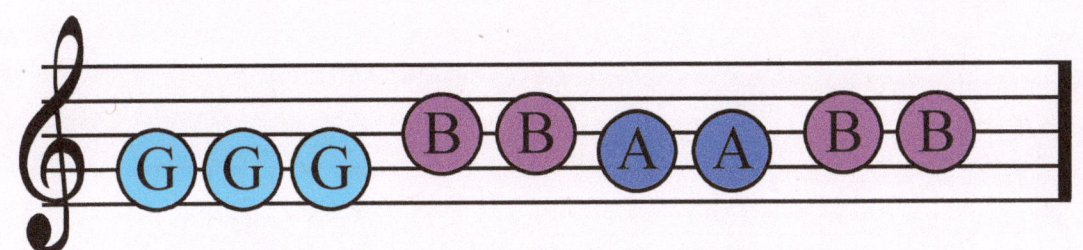

G G G B B A A B B

Ba - by - lon's fal - ling, fal - ling, fal - ling

G G G B B B A A G

Ba - by - lon's fal - ling to rise no more.

Christ Was Born on Christmas Day

Christ was born on Christmas day:
(G E C E G A G)

Wreathe the hol - ly, twine the bay,
(G E C E G A G)

Chris - tus na - tus ho - di - e, the
(F F F G F E D G)

Babe, the Son, the Ho - ly One of Ma - ry.
(G E C F E E D E C C)

Elijah Rock

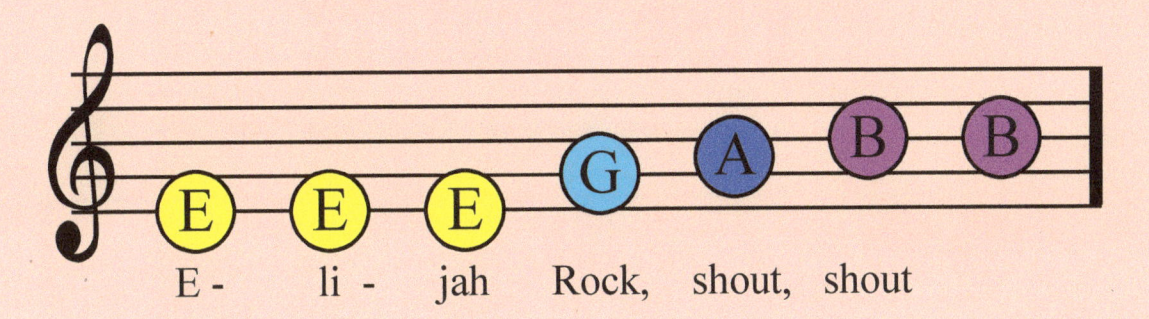

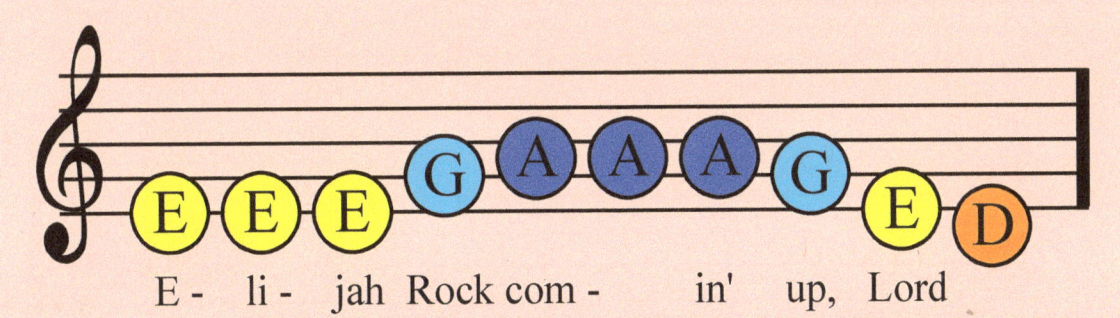

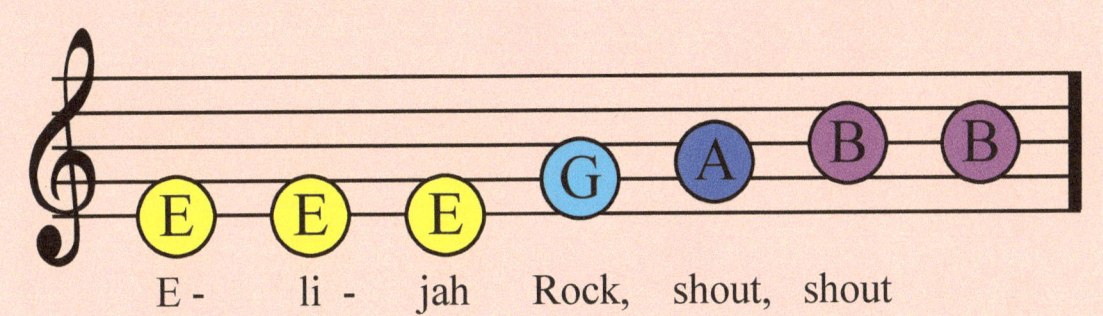

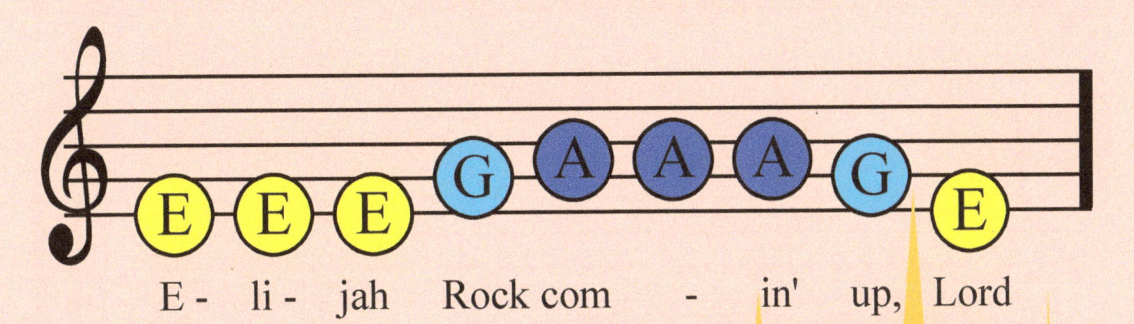

E - E - E G A B B
E - li - jah Rock, shout, shout

E - E - E G A A A G E D
E - li - jah Rock com - in' up, Lord

E - E - E G A B B
E - li - jah Rock, shout, shout

E - E - E G A A A G E
E - li - jah Rock com - in' up, Lord

Every Time I Feel the Spirit

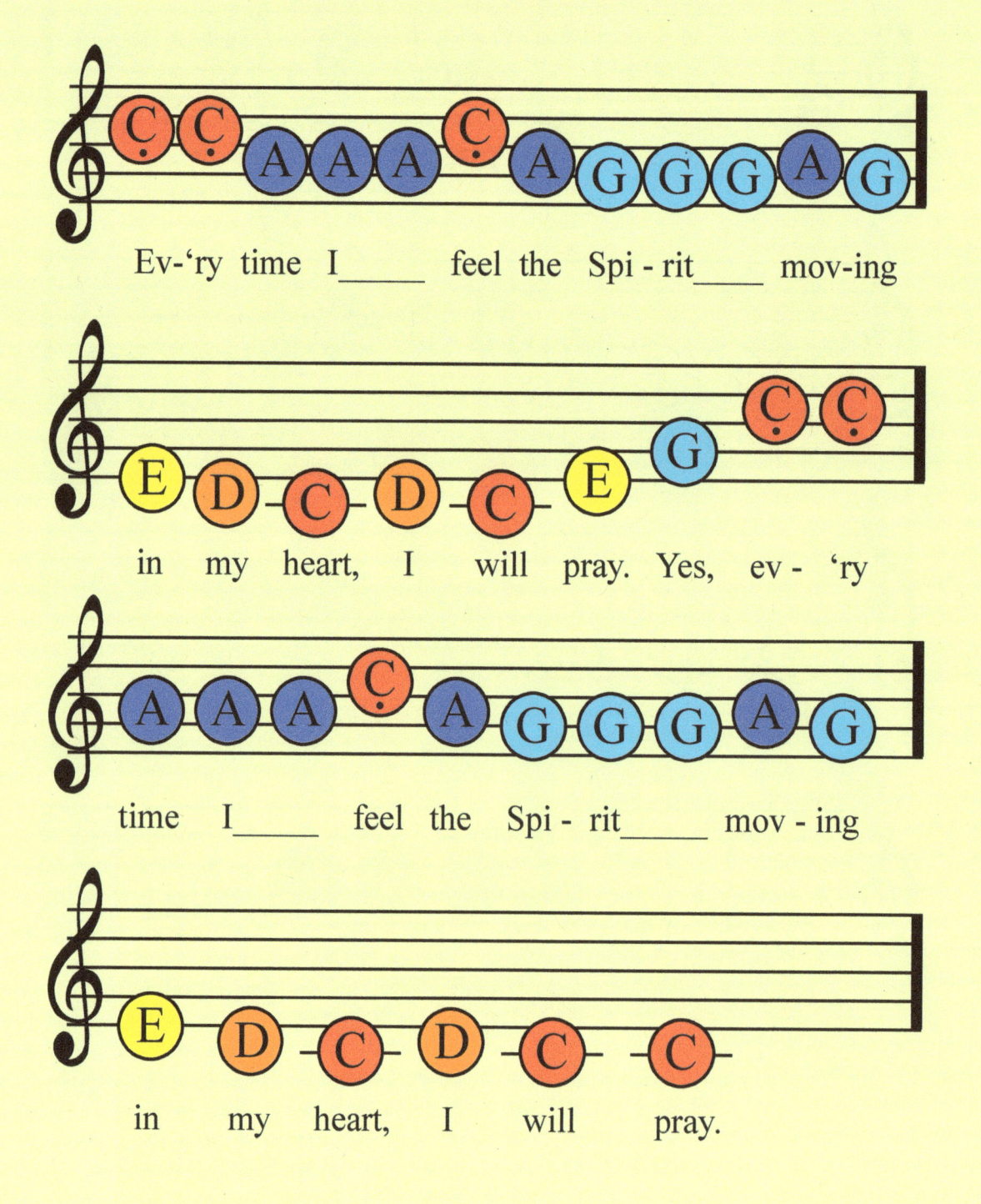

C C A A A C A G G G A G

Ev-'ry time I____ feel the Spi - rit____ mov-ing

E D C D C E G C C

in my heart, I will pray. Yes, ev - 'ry

A A A C A G G G A G

time I____ feel the Spi - rit____ mov - ing

E D C D C C

in my heart, I will pray.

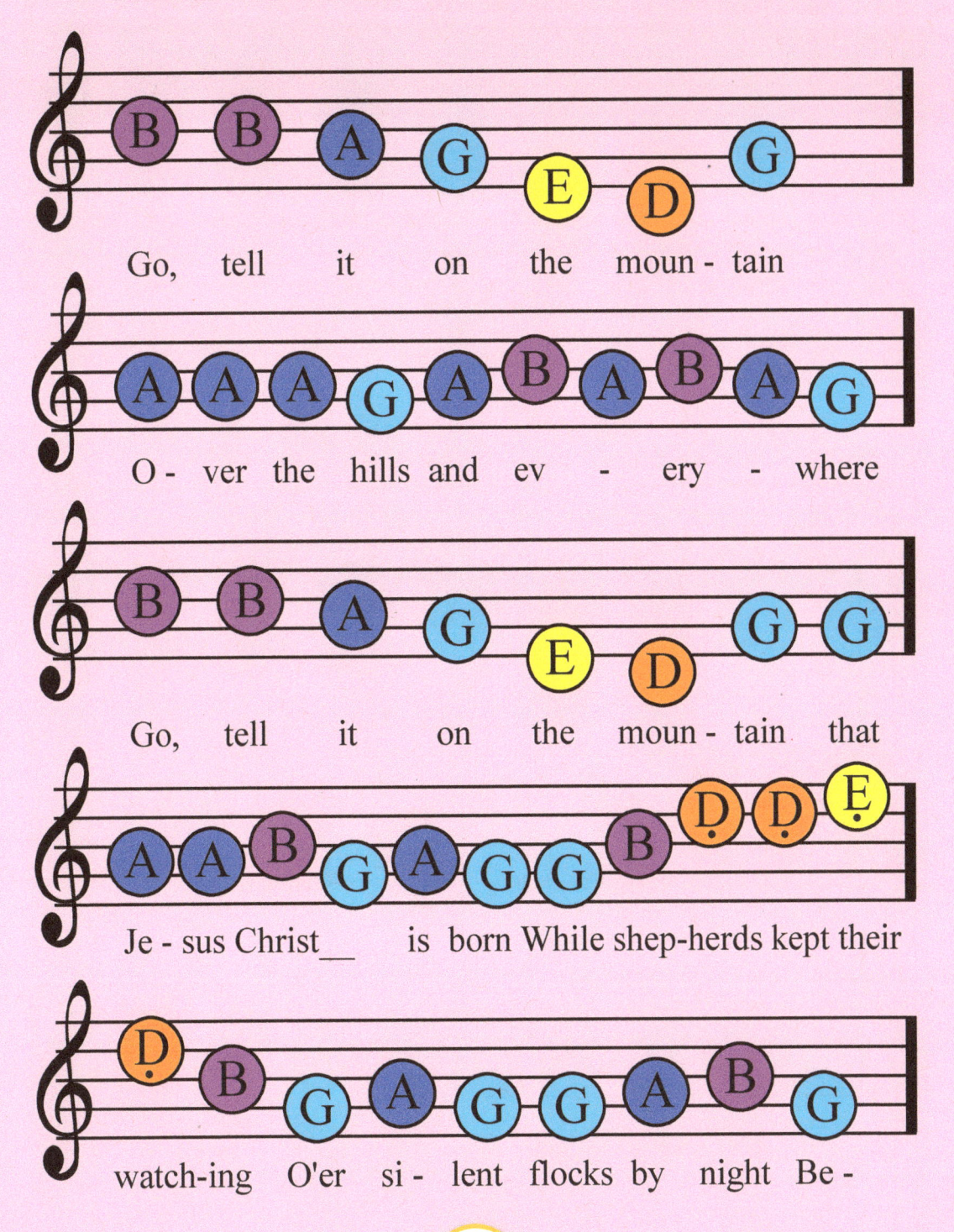

Go, Tell It on the Mountain

B B A G E D G
Go, tell it on the moun - tain

A A A G A B A B A G
O - ver the hills and ev - ery - where

B B A G E D G G
Go, tell it on the moun - tain that

A A B G A G G B D D E
Je - sus Christ__ is born While shep-herds kept their

D B G A G G A B G
watch-ing O'er si - lent flocks by night Be -

36

hold throughout the heav - ens There shone a   Ho - ly

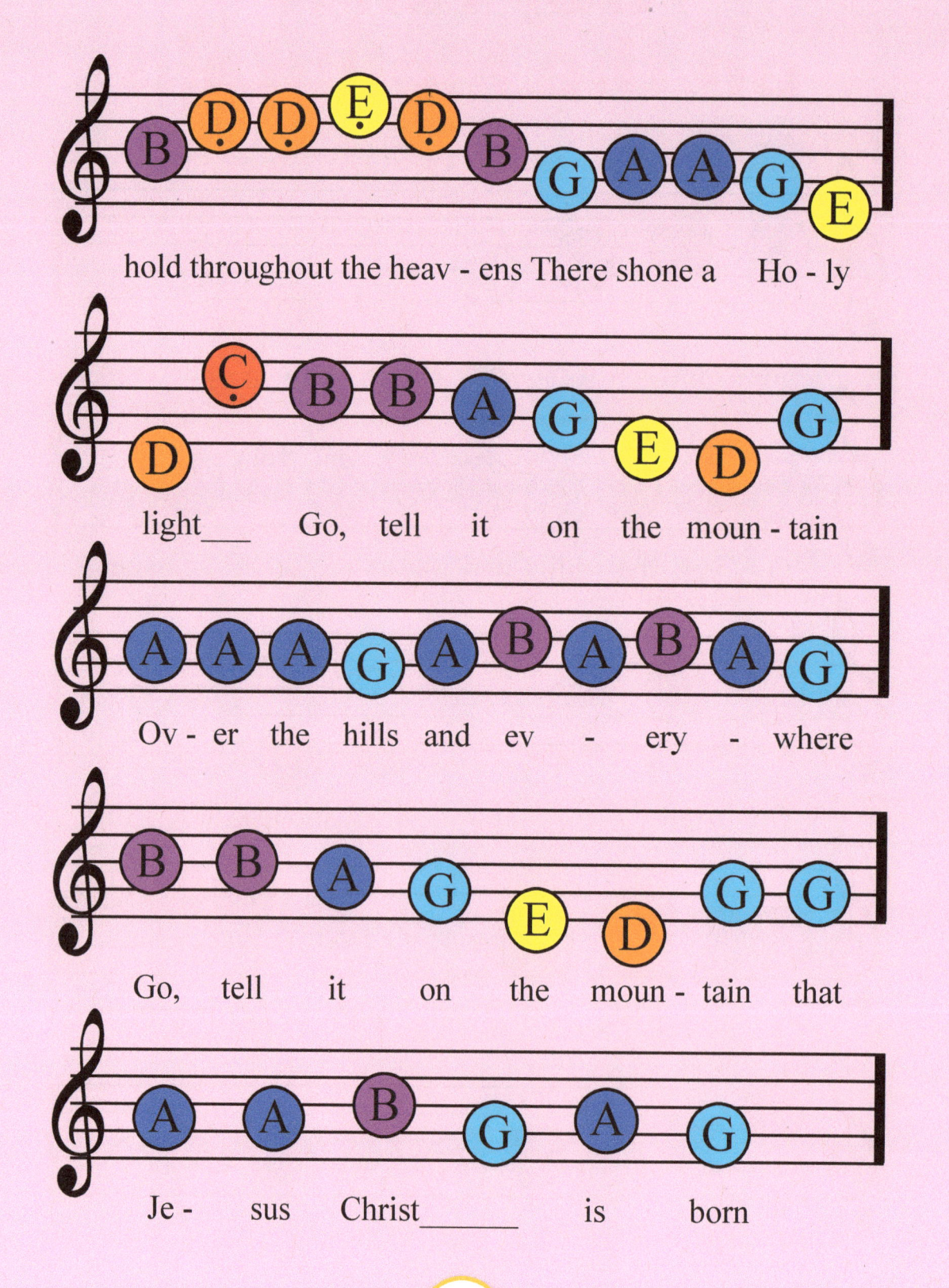

light___   Go,   tell   it   on   the moun - tain

Ov - er   the   hills   and   ev - ery - where

Go,   tell   it   on   the moun - tain that

Je - sus   Christ_____ is   born

God is So Good

C C E D D D F E
God is so good God is so good

E E G F D F E D C
God is so good He's so good to me

He cares for me
He cares for me
He cares for me
He is so good to me

I love him so Hallelujah
I love him so Hallelujah
I love his so Hallelujah
He is so good to me

God is so good
He's so good to me
God, You're so good
You're so good to me

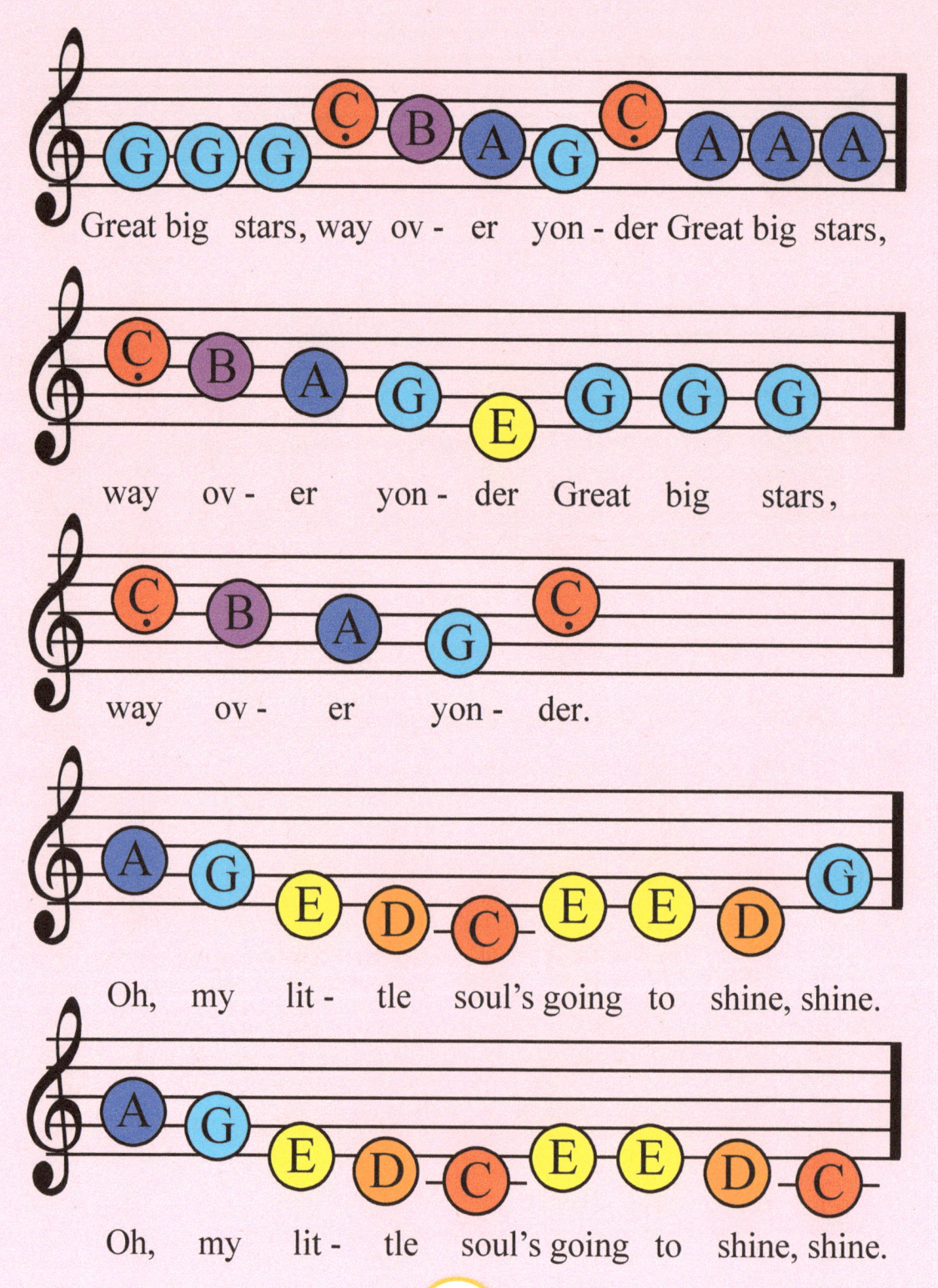

Great Big Stars

Great big stars, way ov - er yon - der Great big stars,

way ov - er yon - der Great big stars,

way ov - er yon - der.

Oh, my lit - tle soul's going to shine, shine.

Oh, my lit - tle soul's going to shine, shine.

Great Day

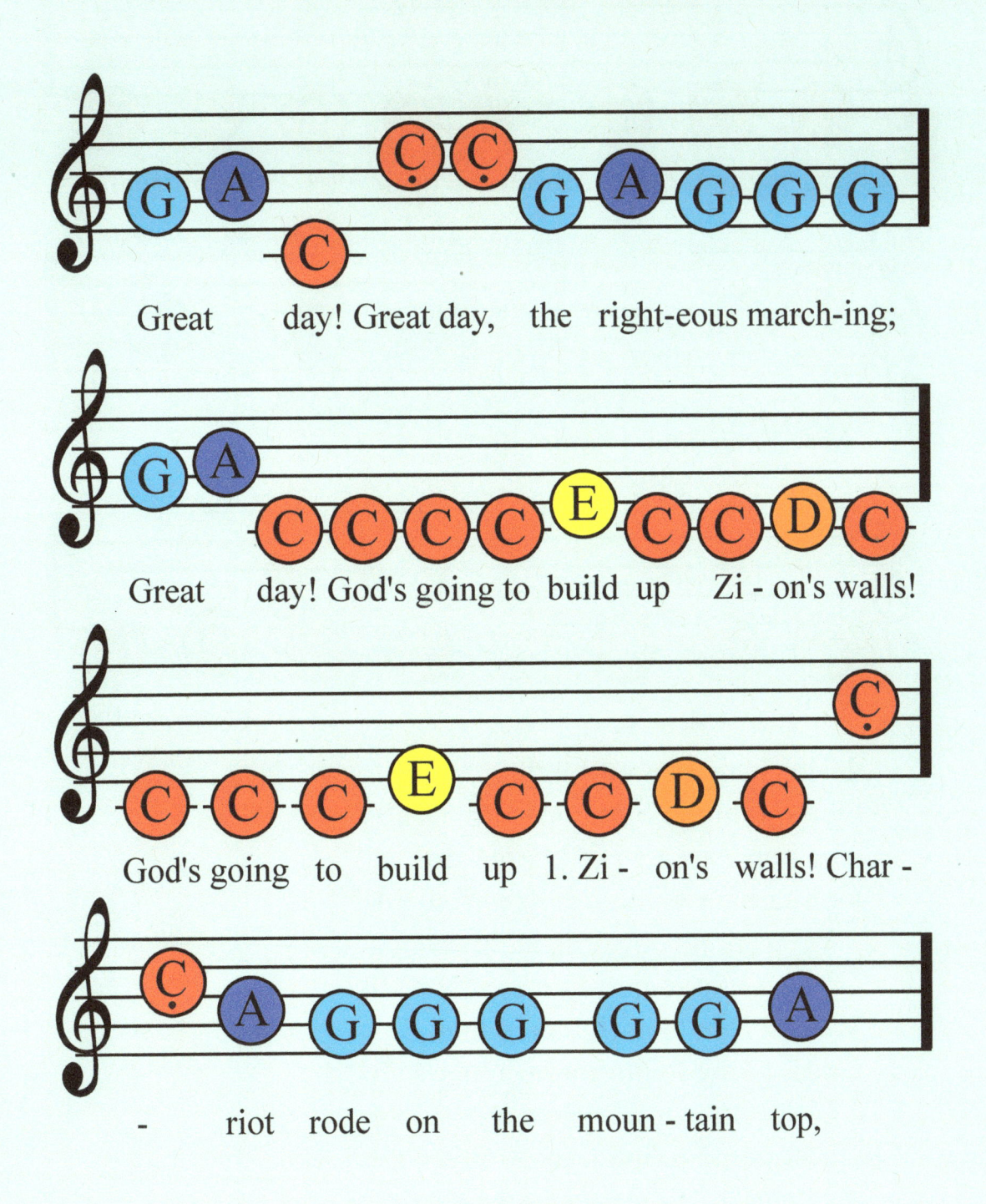

Great day! Great day, the right-eous march-ing;

Great day! God's going to build up Zi - on's walls!

God's going to build up 1. Zi - on's walls! Char -

- riot rode on the moun - tain top,

God's going to build up Zi-on's walls!

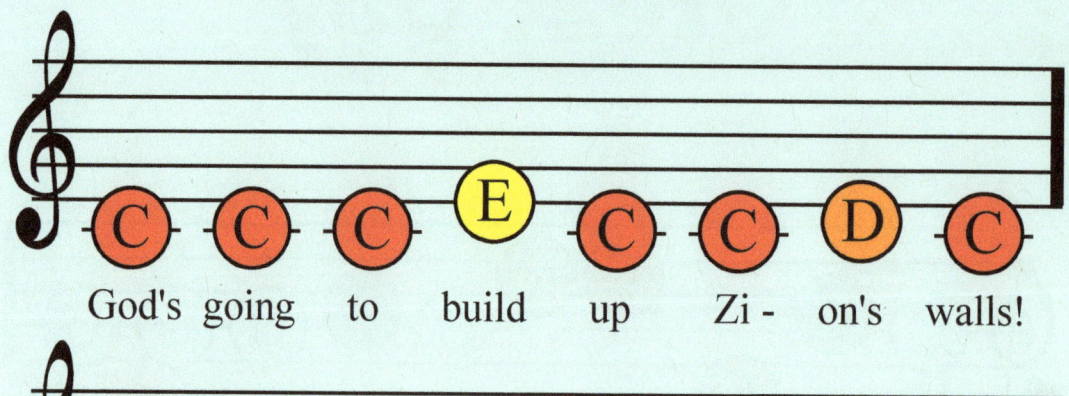

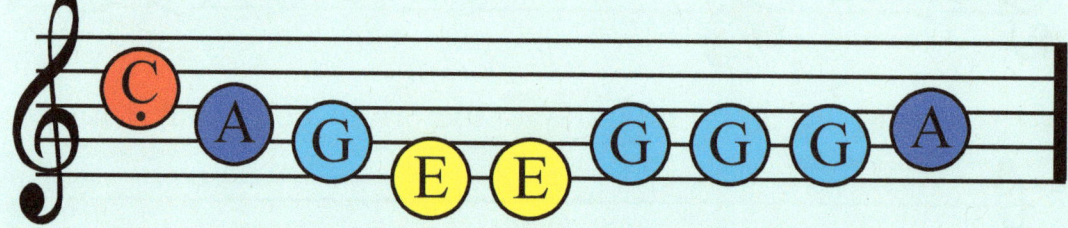

My God spoke and the char-iot did stop,

God's going to build up Zi-on's walls!

2 This is the day of jubilee,
God's going to build up Zion's walls!
The Lord has set His people free,
God's going to build up Zion's walls!
3 We want no cowards in our band,
God's going to build up Zion's walls!
We call for valiant-hearted men,
God's going to build up Zion's walls!
4 Goin't 'take my breastplate, sword and shield,
God's going to build up Zion's walls!
And march out boldly in the field,
God's going to build up Zion's walls!

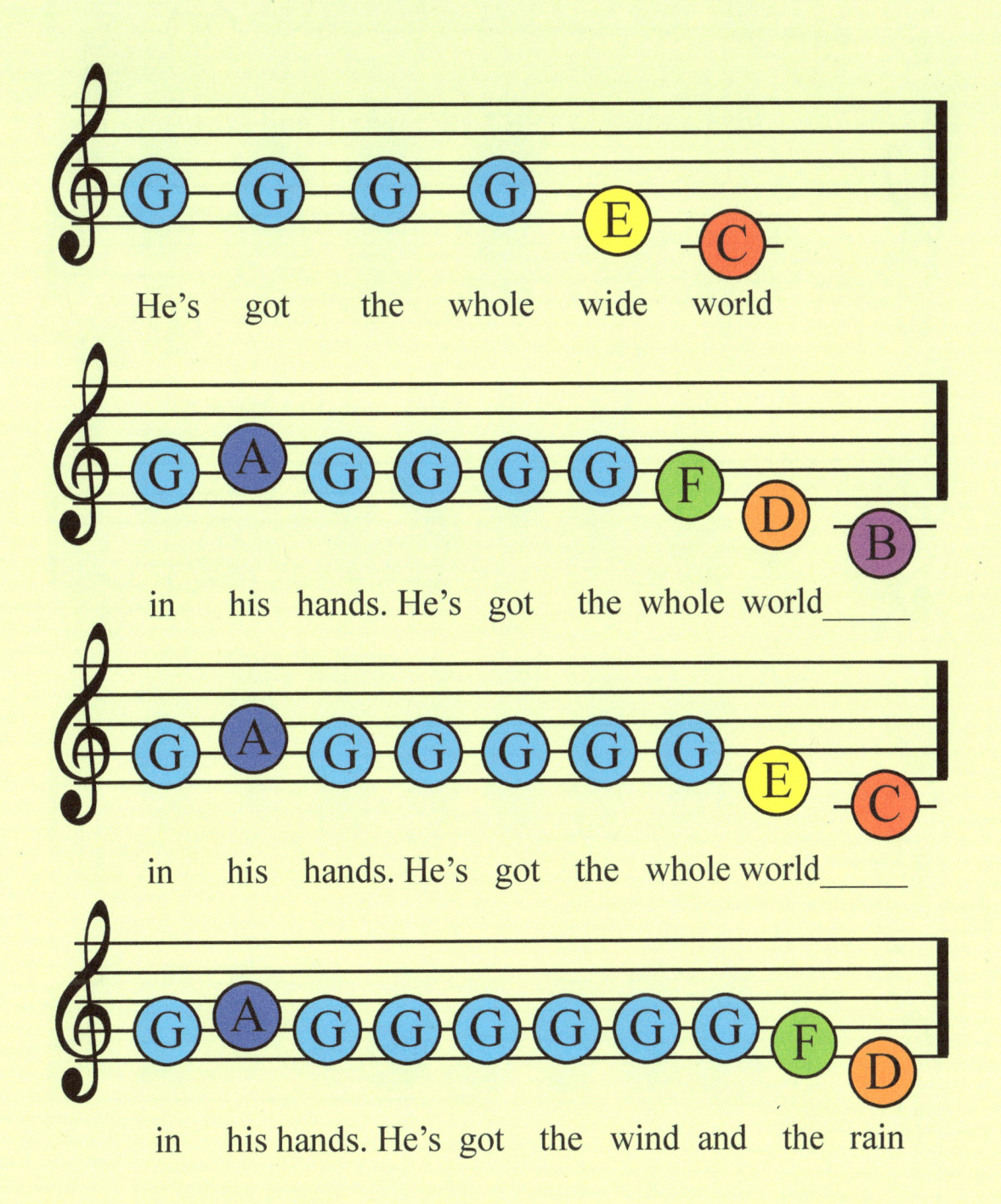

He's Got the Whole World in His Hands

He's got the whole wide world

in his hands. He's got the whole world____

in his hands. He's got the whole world____

in his hands. He's got the wind and the rain

in his hands. He's got the wind and the rain

in his hands. He's got the wind and the rain

in his hands. He's got the wind and the rain

in his hands. He's got the whole world in his

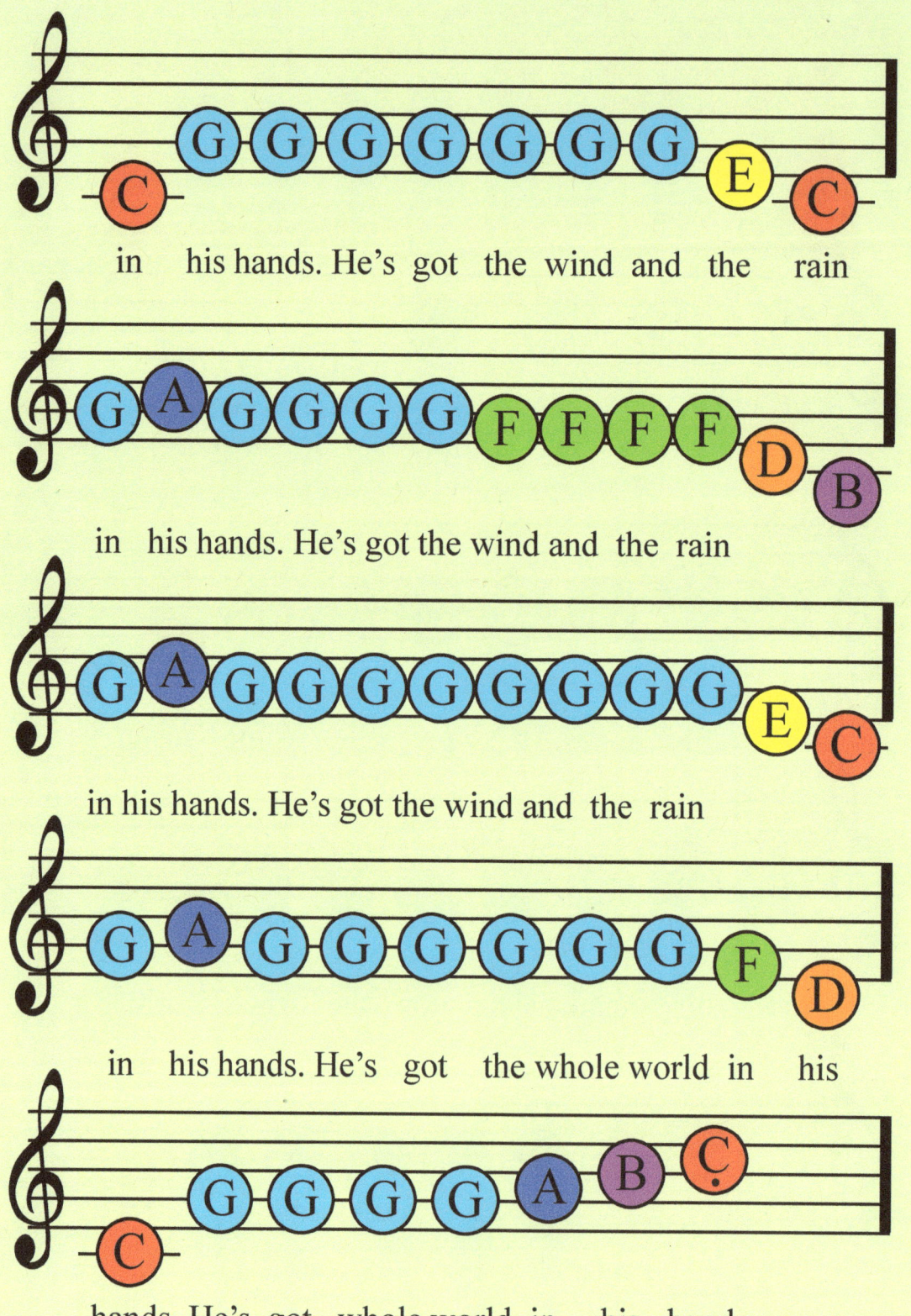

hands. He's got whole world in his hands.

Holy, Holy, Holy

Reginald Heber

Ho - ly, ho - ly, ho - ly! Lord God Al - might - y! Ear - ly in the morn - ing our song shall rise to Thee; Ho - ly, ho - ly, ho - ly, mer - ci - ful and might - y!

God in three Per - sons, blessed Tri - ni - ty!

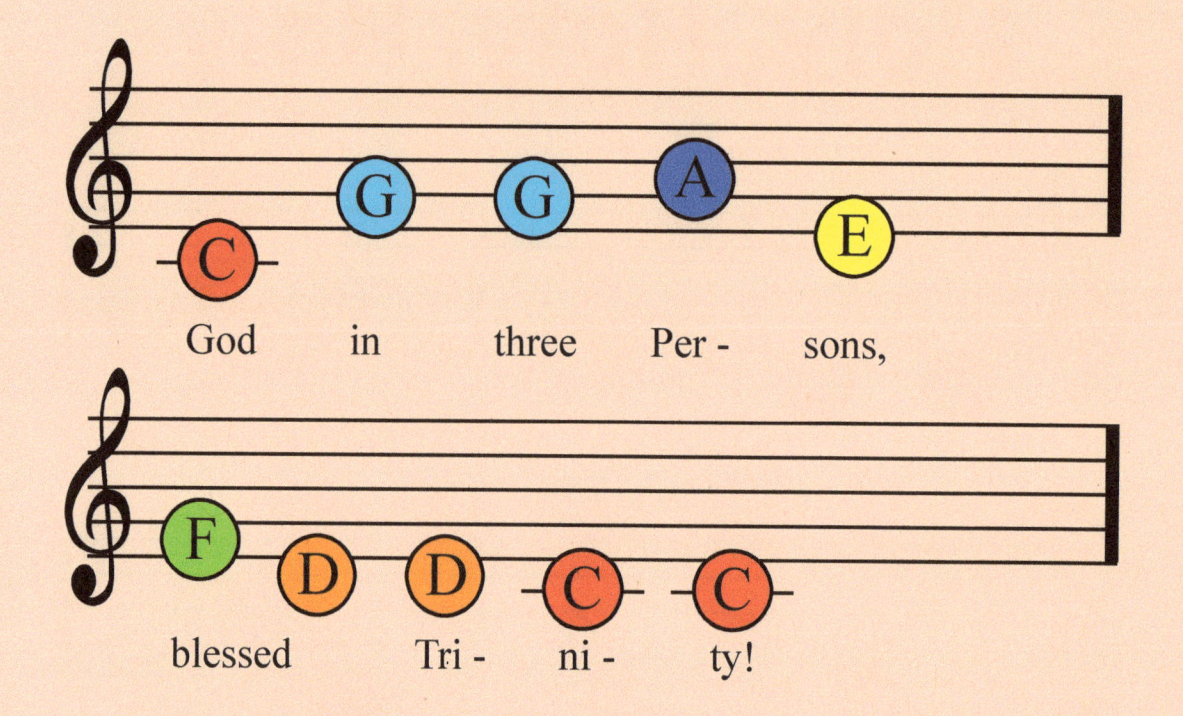

Holy, holy, holy! All the saints adore Thee,
Casting down their golden crowns around the glassy sea;
Cherubim and seraphim falling down before Thee,
Who was, and is, and evermore shall be.

Holy, holy, holy! though the darkness hide Thee,
Through the eye of sinful man Thy glory may not see;
Only Thou art holy; there is none beside Thee,
Perfect in power, in love, and purity.

Holy, holy, holy! Lord God Almighty!
All Thy works shall praise Thy Name,
in earth, and sky, and sea;
Holy, holy, holy; merciful and mighty!
God in three Persons, blessed Trinity!

I've Got the Joy, Joy, Joy

George William Cooke

I've got the joy, joy, joy, joy. Down in my heart (where?)

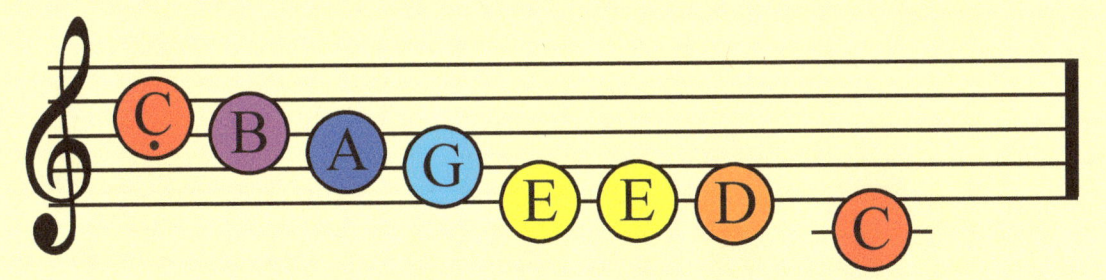

Down in my heart, Down in my heart, I've got the

joy, joy, joy, joy. Down in my heart (where?)

Down in my heart to stay. I've got the

46

love   of   Je - sus,   love   of   Je - sus

Down in my heart (where?). Down in my heart (where?)

Down   in   my   heart.   I've   got   the   love

of   Je - sus,   love   of   Je - sus.   Down   in

my   heart (where?).   Down   in   my   heart   to   stay

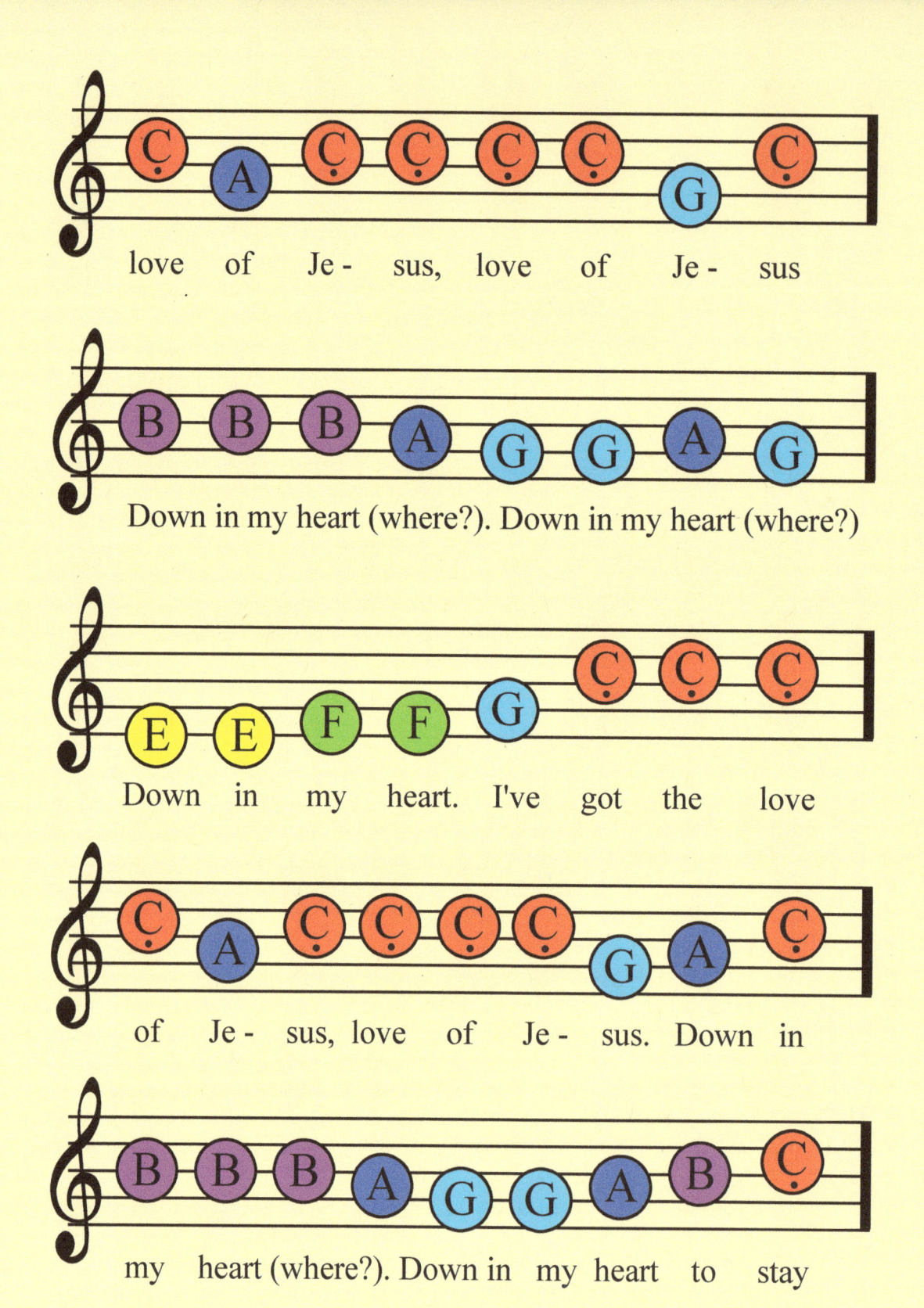

Peace Like a River

C D F F G A A A G
I've got peace like a river, I've got

F F F D C C D F F G
peace like a river, I've got peace like a

A A G F G C D F F G
river in my soul. I've got peace like a

A A A G F F F D C C D
river, I've got peace like a river, I've got

F F G A A G G F
peace like a river in my soul.

48

Jesus Loves Me

Anna Bartlett Warner, William B. Bradbury

Je - sus loves me, this I know,

For the Bi - ble tells me so. Lit - tle ones to

Him belong. They are weak but He is strong.

Yes, Je - sus loves me, Yes, Je - sus loves me,

Yes, Je - sus loves me, the
Bi - ble tells me so.

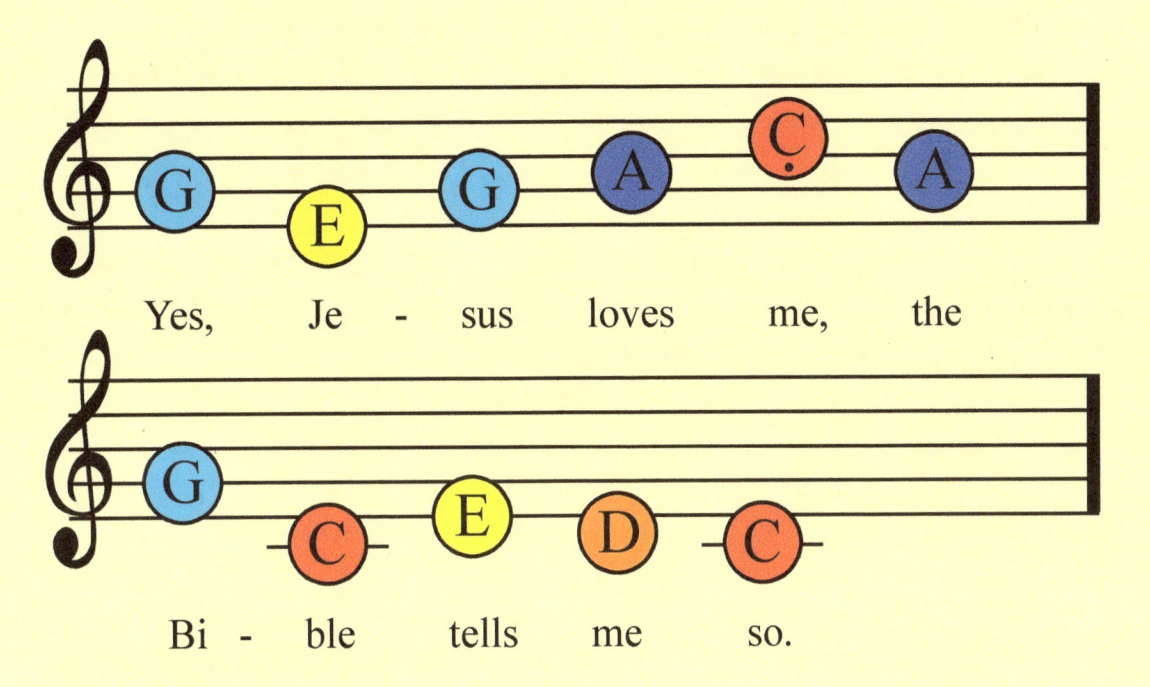

Jesus loves me, how can it be
That the only Son of God should care for me
To take away my sin and set me free
To take my life and make it all it's meant to be

Jesus loves me, this I know
It's not just the Bible that tells me so
I can feel it, feel it in my soul
Jesus loves me, this I know

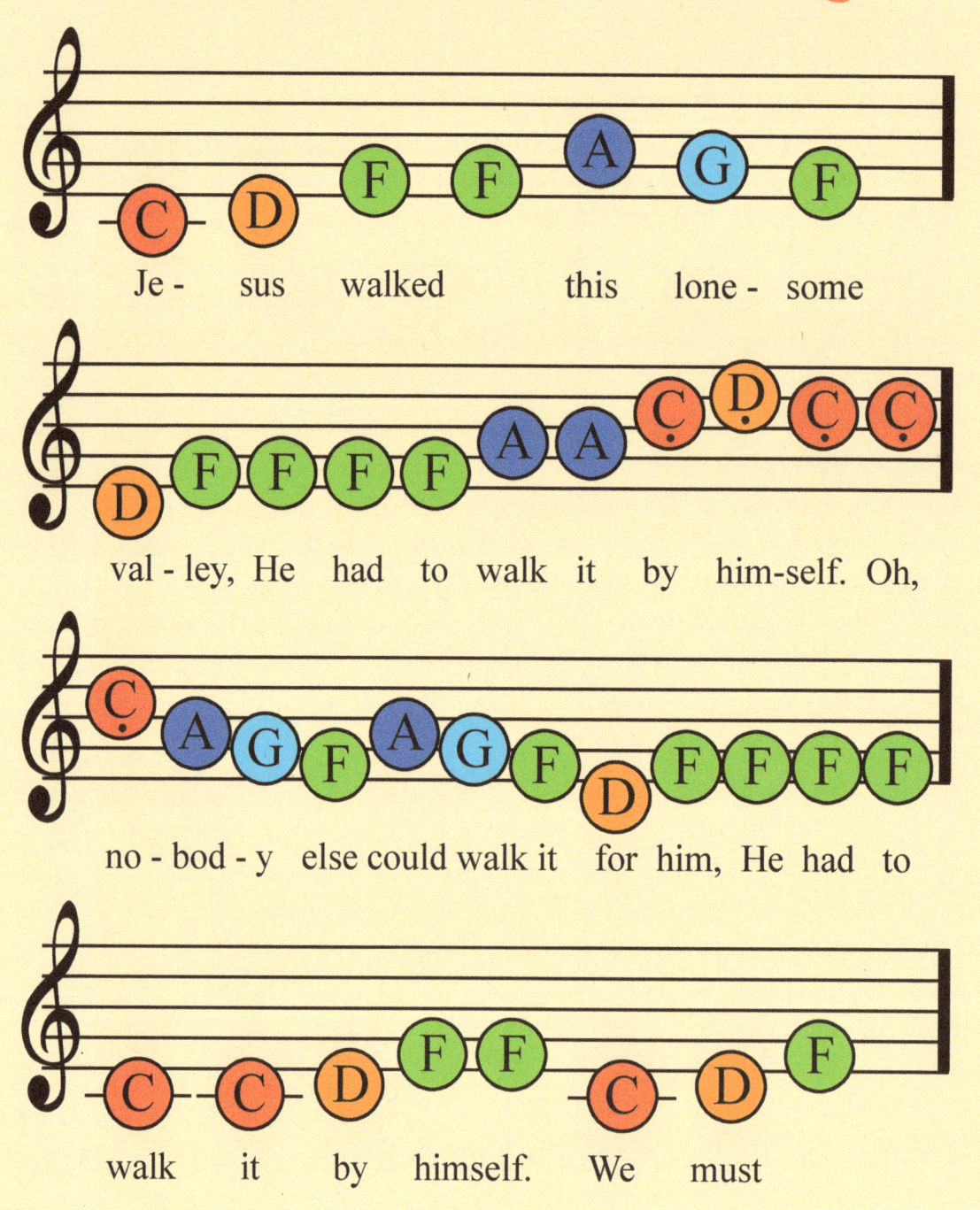

Jesus Walked this Lonesome Valley

Je - sus walked this lone - some val - ley, He had to walk it by him-self. Oh, no - bod - y else could walk it for him, He had to walk it by himself. We must

Joy to the World!

Isaac Watts, George Frederic Handel

C B A G F E D C G
Joy to the world, the Lord is come! Let

A A B B C C C B A G
earth re - ceive her King; let ev - 'ry

G F E C C B A G
heart pre - pare him

G F E E E E E E F
room and heav'n and na - ture

G F E D D D D E F E D
sing, and heav'n and na - ture sing, and

52

C A G F E F E D C

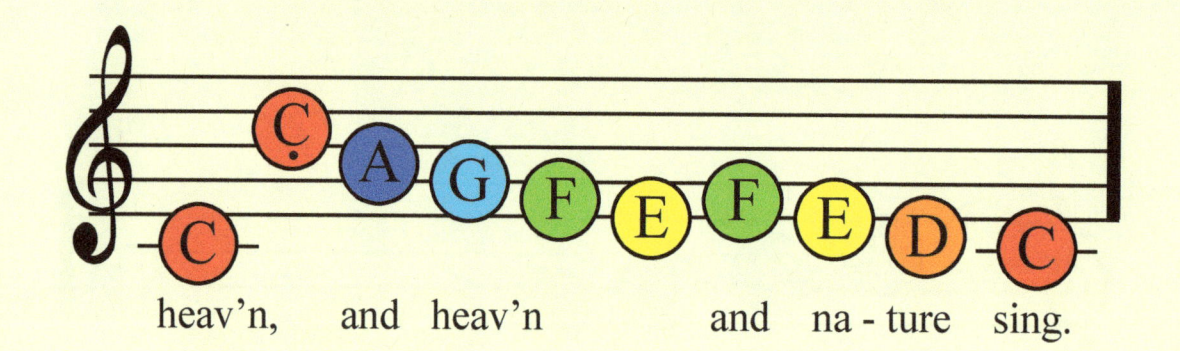

heav'n, and heav'n and na-ture sing.

Joy to the earth, the Savior reigns!
Let men their songs employ,
while fields and floods, rocks, hills, and plains,
repeat the sounding joy,
repeat the sounding joy,
repeat, repeat the sounding joy

No more let sins and sorrows grow
nor thorns infest the ground;
he comes to make his blessings flow
far as the curse is found,
far as the curse is found,
far as, far as the curse is found

Just As I Am

Charlotte Elliott, William B. Bradbury

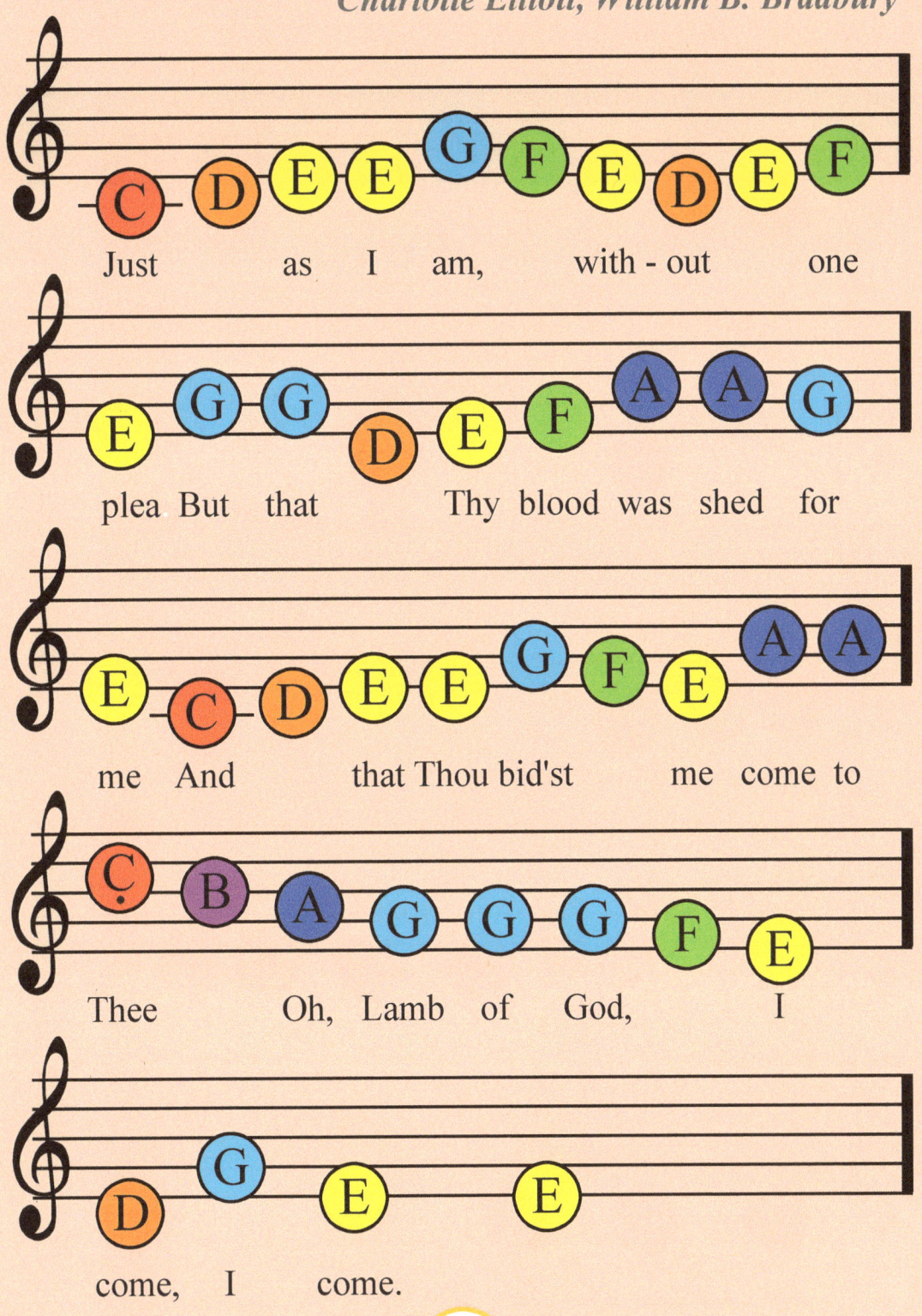

C D E E G F E D E F
Just as I am, with-out one

E G G D E F A A G
plea But that Thy blood was shed for

E C D E E G F E A A
me And that Thou bid'st me come to

C B A G G G F E
Thee Oh, Lamb of God, I

D G E E
come, I come.

54

Kumbaya, My Lord

African-American Spiritual

C E G G G G A A
Kum ba ya my Lord____, kum ba

G G C E G G G G F E
ya____ Kum ba ya my Lord____, kum ba

D D C E G G G G A A
ya____ Kum ba ya my Lord____, kum ba

G G F E C C D D
ya____ Oh Lord_____, kum ba

C C C E
ya_____ Someone's

55

Michael Row the Boat Ashore

C E G E G A G E G
Mich - ael row the boat a - shore, hal - le -

A G E G G E F E
lu - jah Mich - ael row the boat a -

D C D E D C
shore, hal - le - lu - jah

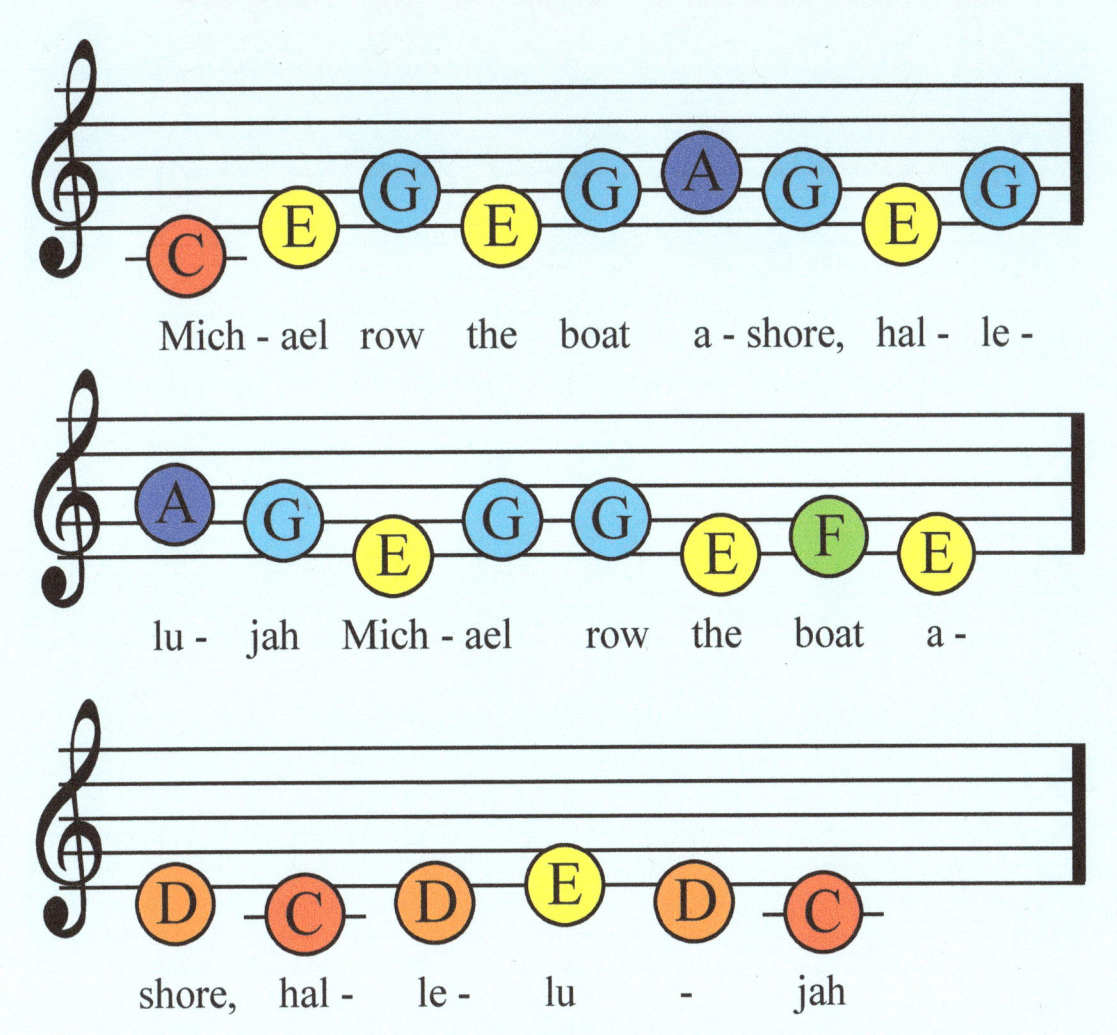

Sister help to trim the sail, hallelujah
Sister help to trim the sail, hallelujah
The river is deep and the river is wide, hallelujah
Green pastures on the other side, hallelujah
Michael row the boat ashore, hallelujah
Michael row the boat ashore, hallelujah

Nobody Knows the Trouble I've Seen

African-American Spiritual

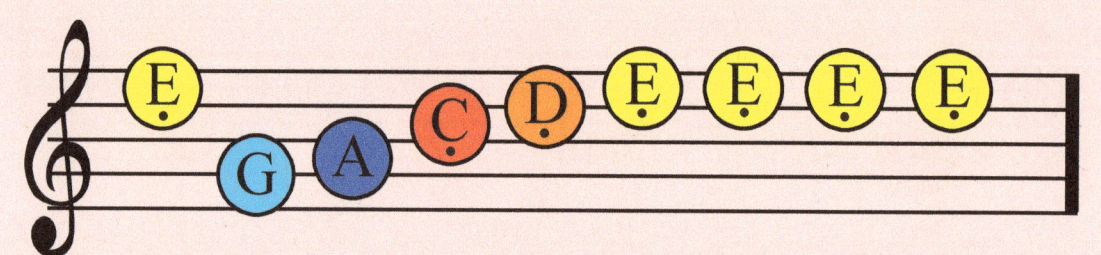

E G A C D E E E E
No - bod - y knows the trou - ble I've seen

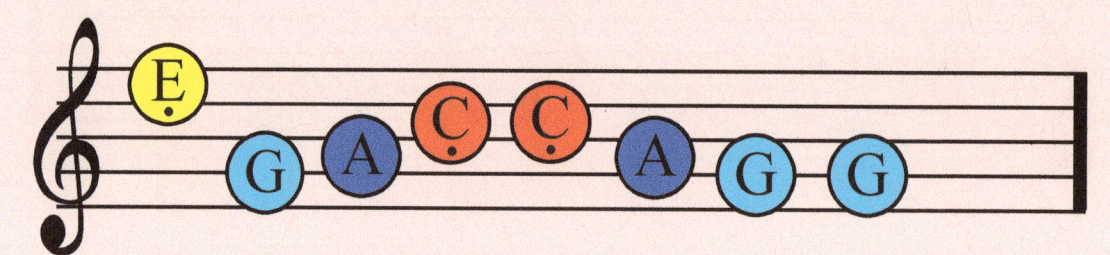

E G A C C A G G
No - bod - y knows my sor - row____

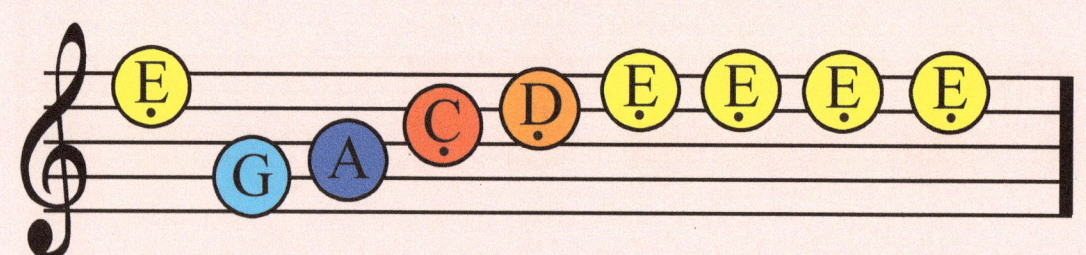

E G A C D E E E E
No - bod - y knows the trou - ble I've seen

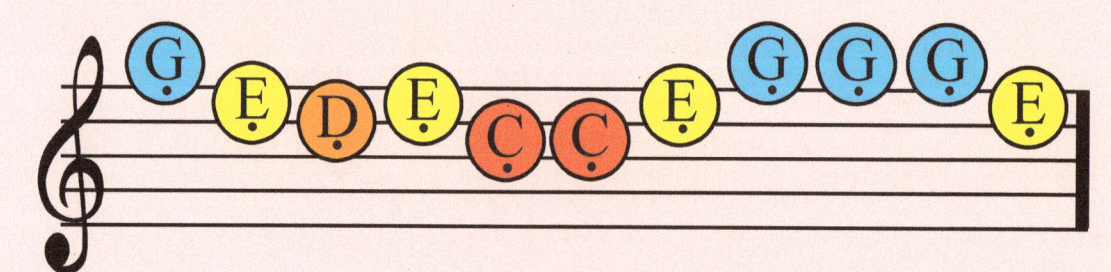

G E D E C C E G G E
Glo - ry, Hal - le - lu - jah Sometimes I'm up Some -

times I'm down Oh, yes, Lord Sometimes I'm al - most

to the ground Oh, yes, Lord Oh, no - bo - dy

knows the trou - ble I've seen No - bo - dy knows my

sor - row____ No - bo - dy knows the trou - ble I've

seen Glo - ry, Hal - le - lu - jah

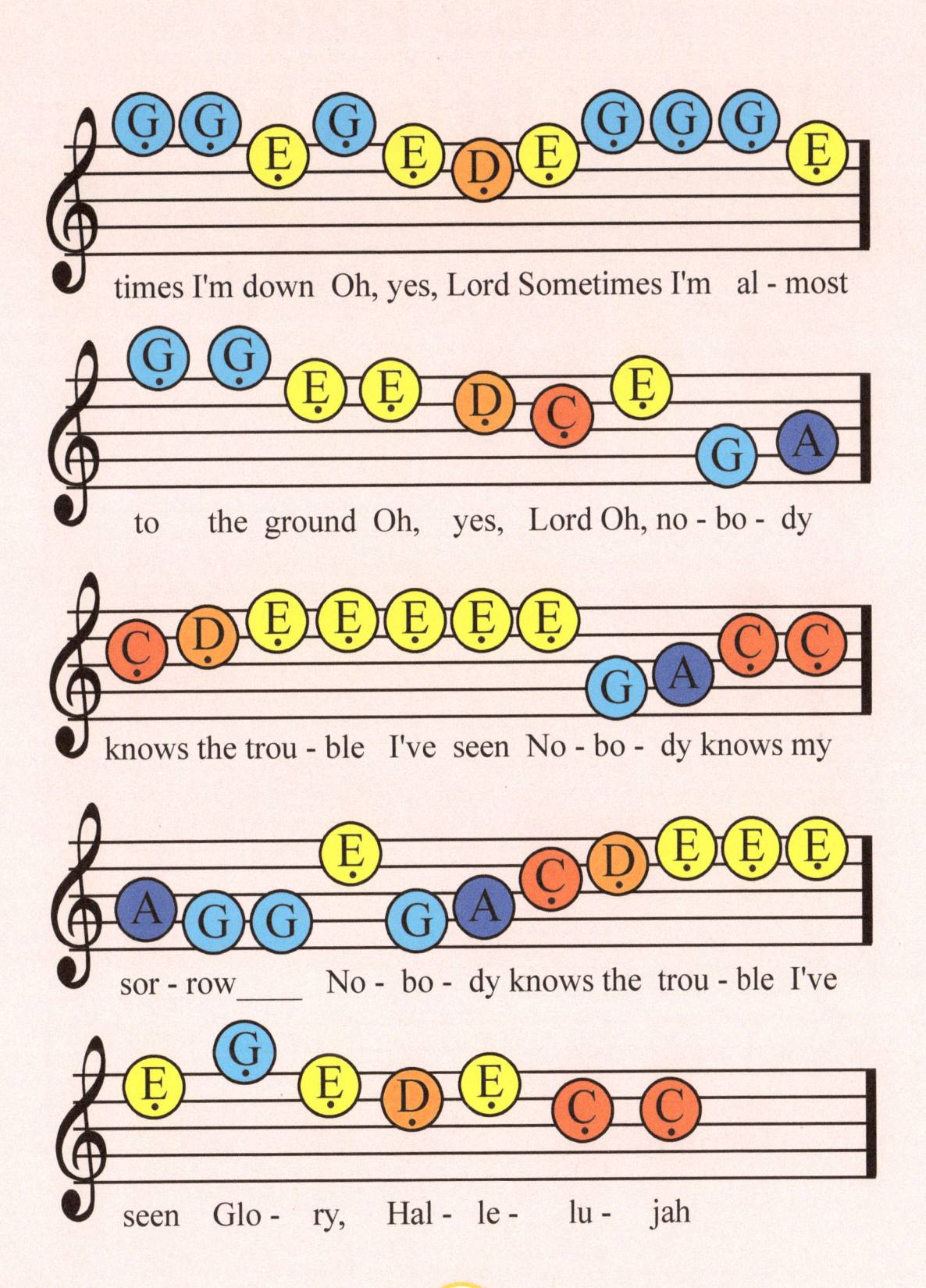

Praise Him, All You Little Children

Carey Bonner

Praise Him, praise Him, all you lit-tle children,

God is love, God is love;

Praise Him, praise Him, all you lit-tle children,

God is love, God is love.

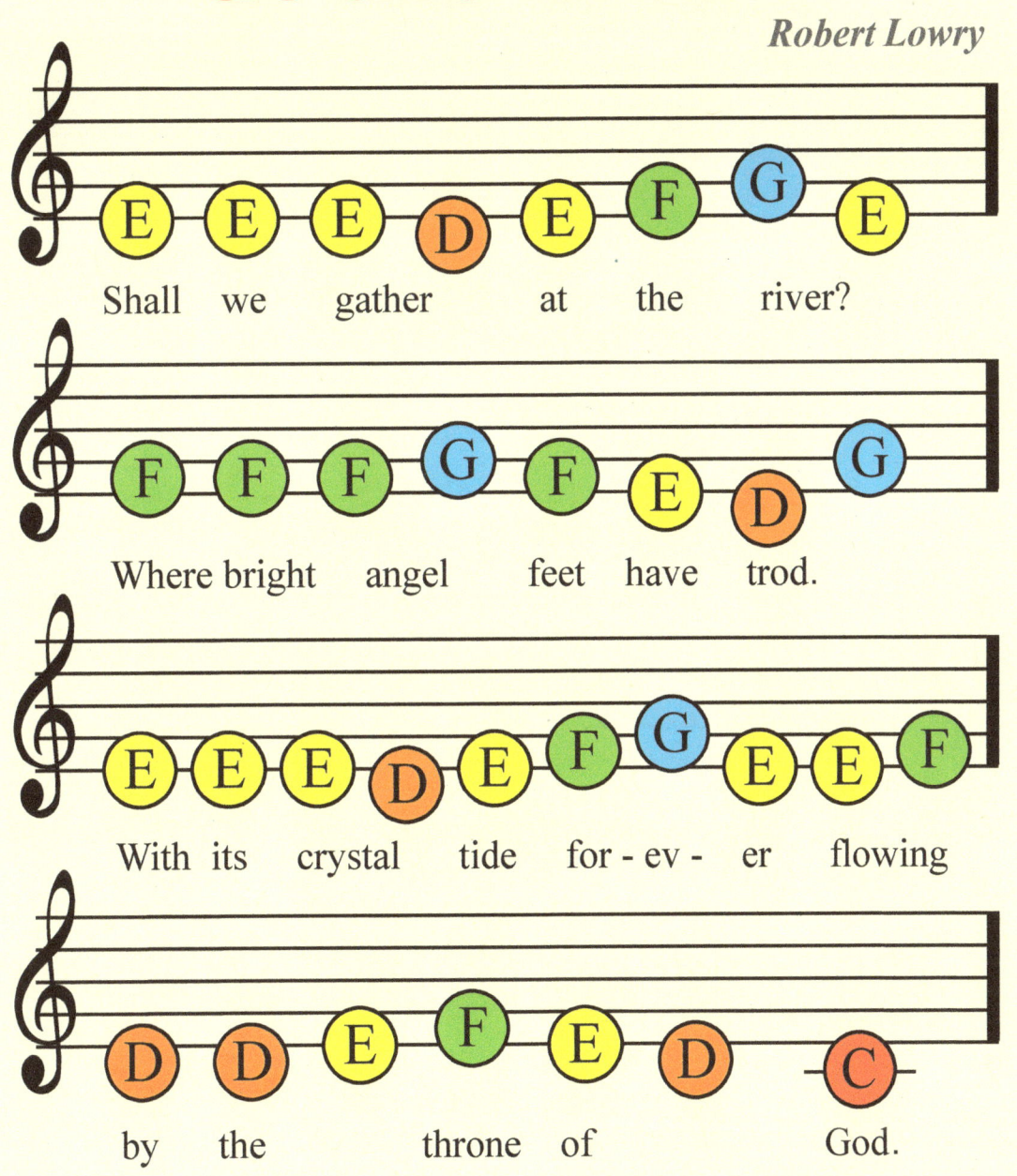

Shall We Gather at the River?

Robert Lowry

E E E D E F G E
Shall we gather at the river?

F F F G F E D G
Where bright angel feet have trod.

E E E D E F G E E F
With its crystal tide for - ev - er flowing

D D E F E D C
by the throne of God.

Yes, we'll gather at the river the beau-ti-ful, the beau-ti-ful river.
Gather with the saints at the river that flows by the throne of God.

Soon we'll reach the shining river,
Soon our pilgrimage will cease,
Soon our happy hearts will quiver
With the melody of peace.
Yes, we'll gather at the river
The beautiful, the beautiful river
Gather with the saints at the river
That flows by the throne of God.

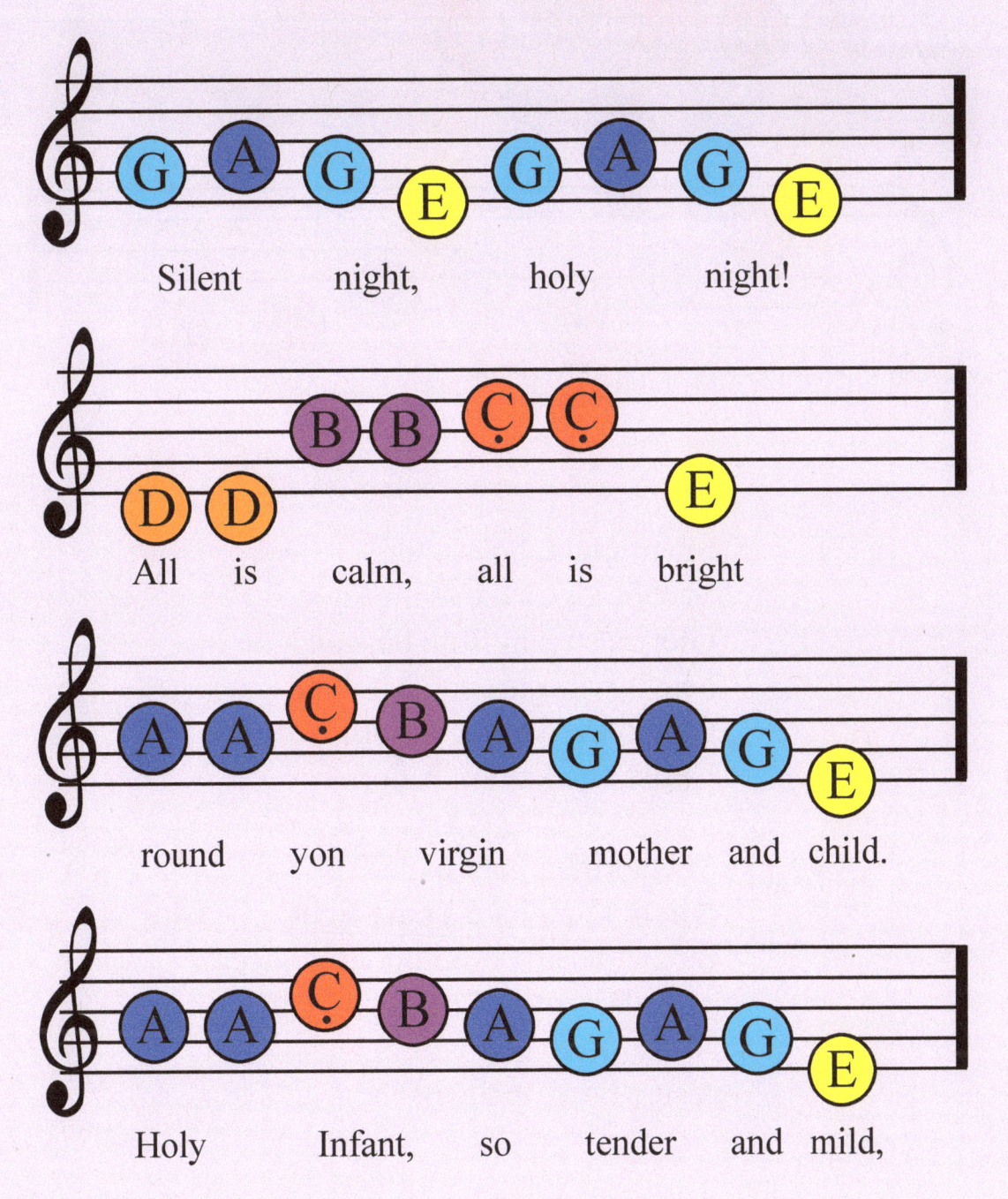

Silent Night, Holy Night

G A G E G A G E
Silent night, holy night!

D D B B C C E
All is calm, all is bright

A A C B A G A G E
round yon virgin mother and child.

A A C B A G A G E
Holy Infant, so tender and mild,

sleep   in   heavenly   peace,

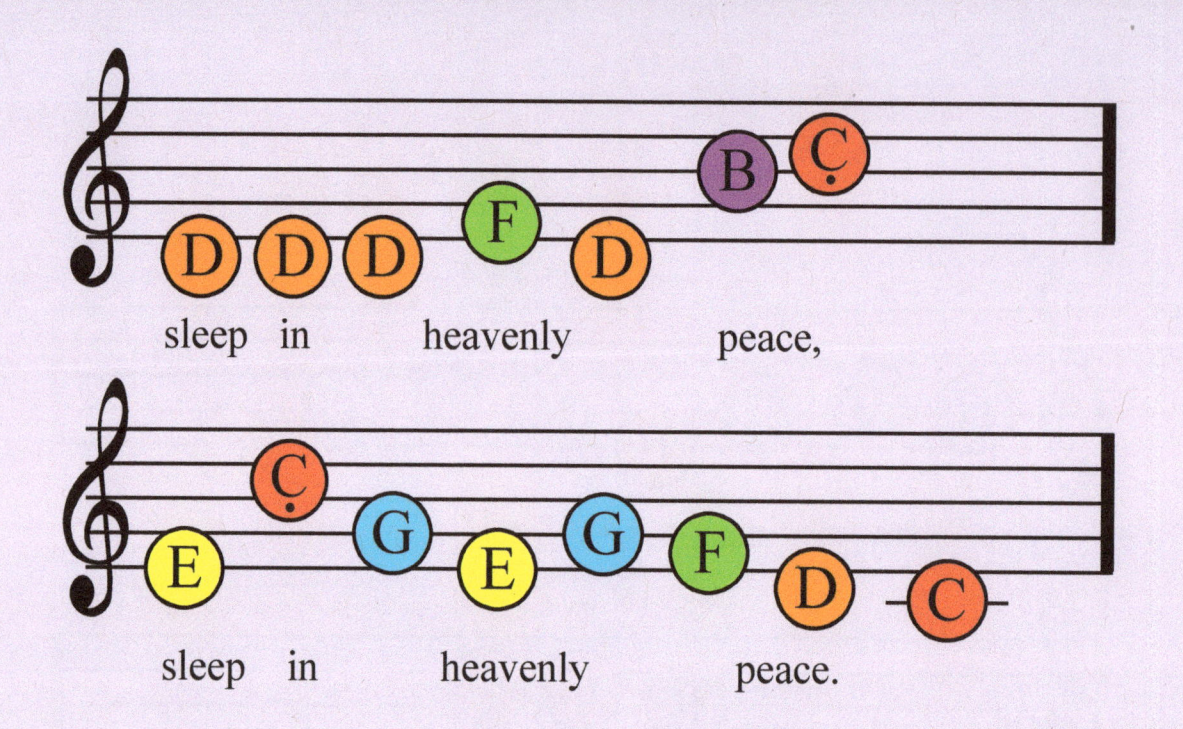

sleep   in   heavenly   peace.

Silent night, holy night!
Shepherds quake at the sight.
Glories stream from heaven afar,
heav'nly hosts sing, Alleluia!
Christ, the Savior, is born!
Christ, the Savior, is born!

Silent night, holy night!
Son of God, love's pure light
radiant beams from thy holy face
with the dawn of redeeming grace,
Jesus, Lord, at thy birth,
Jesus, Lord, at thy birth.

Sinner Man

African-American Spiritual

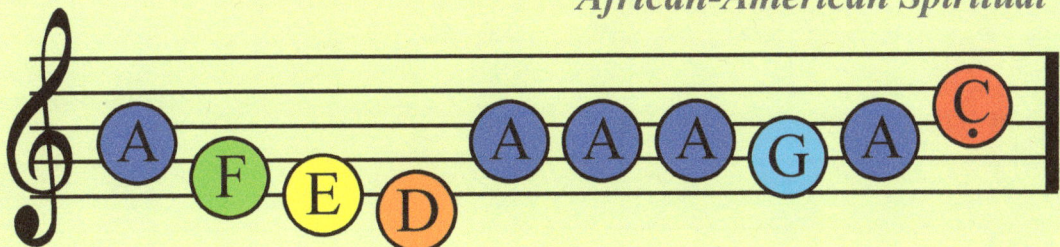

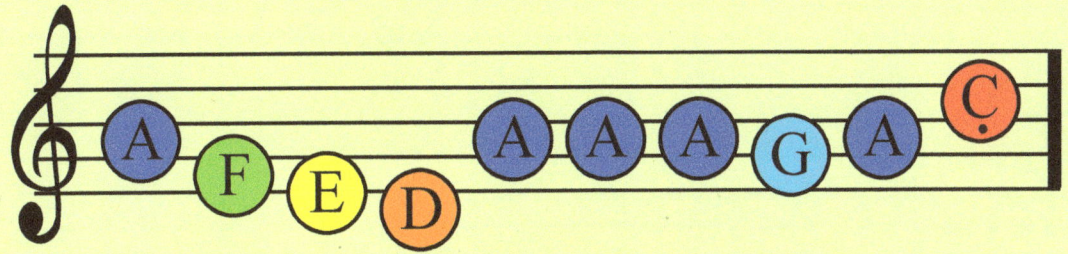

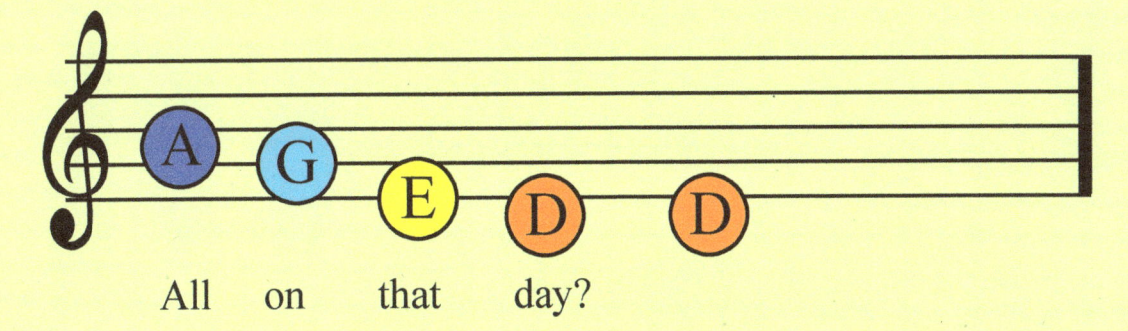

Oh, sin - ner - man, where you gon - na run to?

Oh, sin - ner - man, where you gon - na run to?

Oh, sin - ner - man, where you gon - na run to?

All on that day?

Am I a Soldier of the Cross

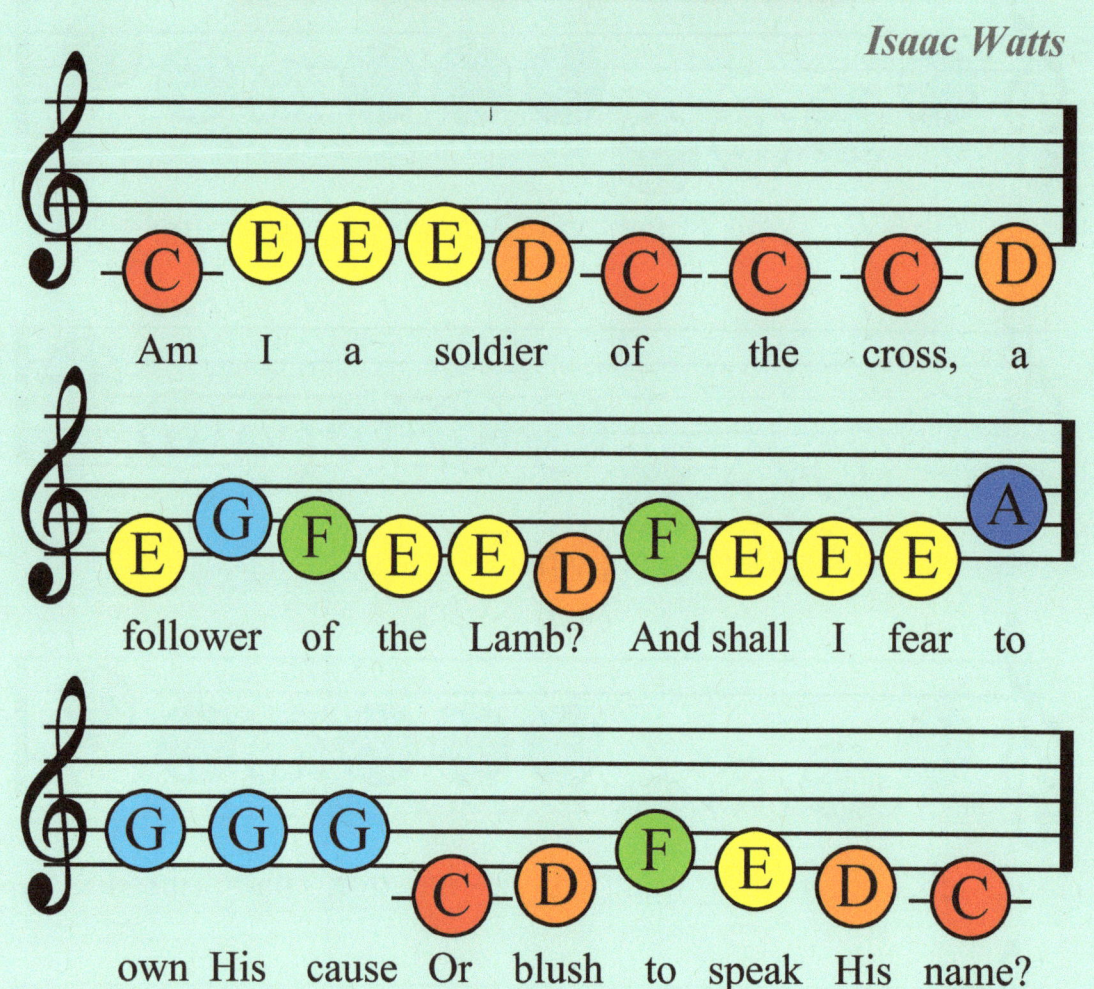

Isaac Watts

Am I a soldier of the cross, a follower of the Lamb? And shall I fear to own His cause Or blush to speak His name?

Sure I must fight if I would reign:
Increase my courage, Lord;
I'll bear the toil, endure the pain,
Supported by Thy word.

Somebody's Knocking at Your Door

African-American Spiritual

F F A G F D F F F
Some - bod - y's knock - ing at your door,____

C C F D C A C C C
Some - bod - y's knock - ing at your door,____

C F D C A A F F D
O____ sin - ner, why don't you an - swer?

F F A G F D F F F
Some - bod - y's knock - ing at your door,____

O____ sin - ner, why don't you an - swer?

Some - bod - y's knock - ing at your door

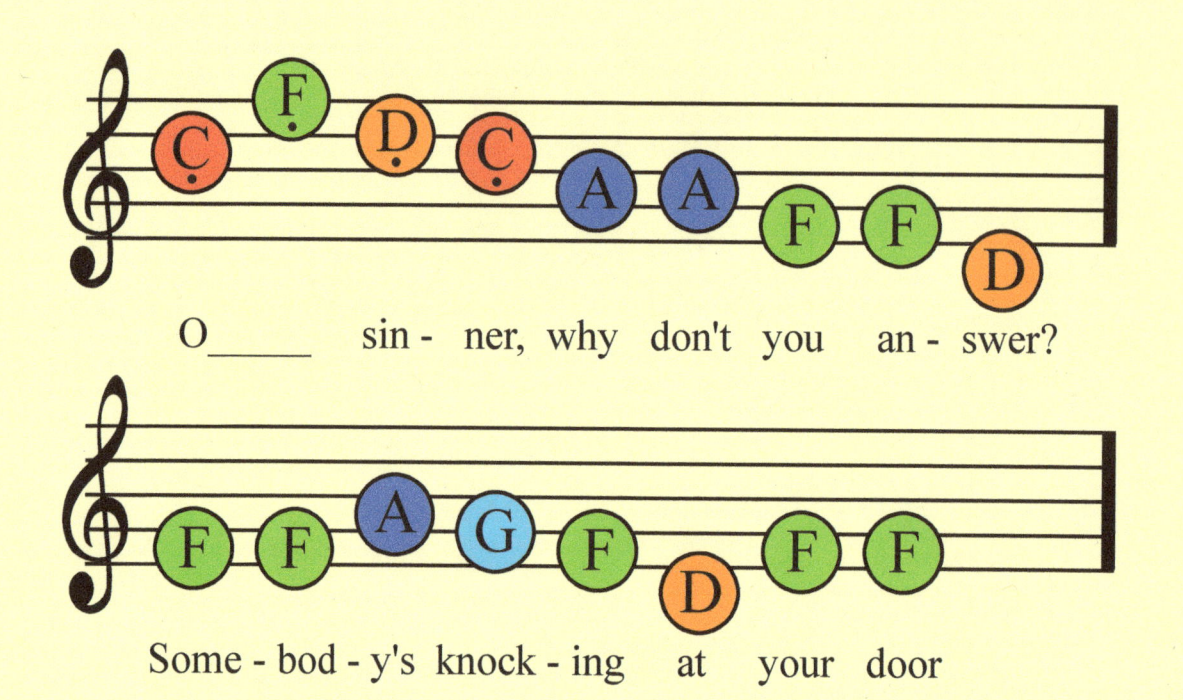

Knocks like Jesus,
Somebody's knocking at your door.

Can't you hear Him?
Somebody's knocking at your door.

Answer Jesus,
Somebody's knocking at your door.

Jesus calls you,
Somebody's knocking at your door.

Can't you trust Him?
Somebody's knocking at your door.

Song of Praise

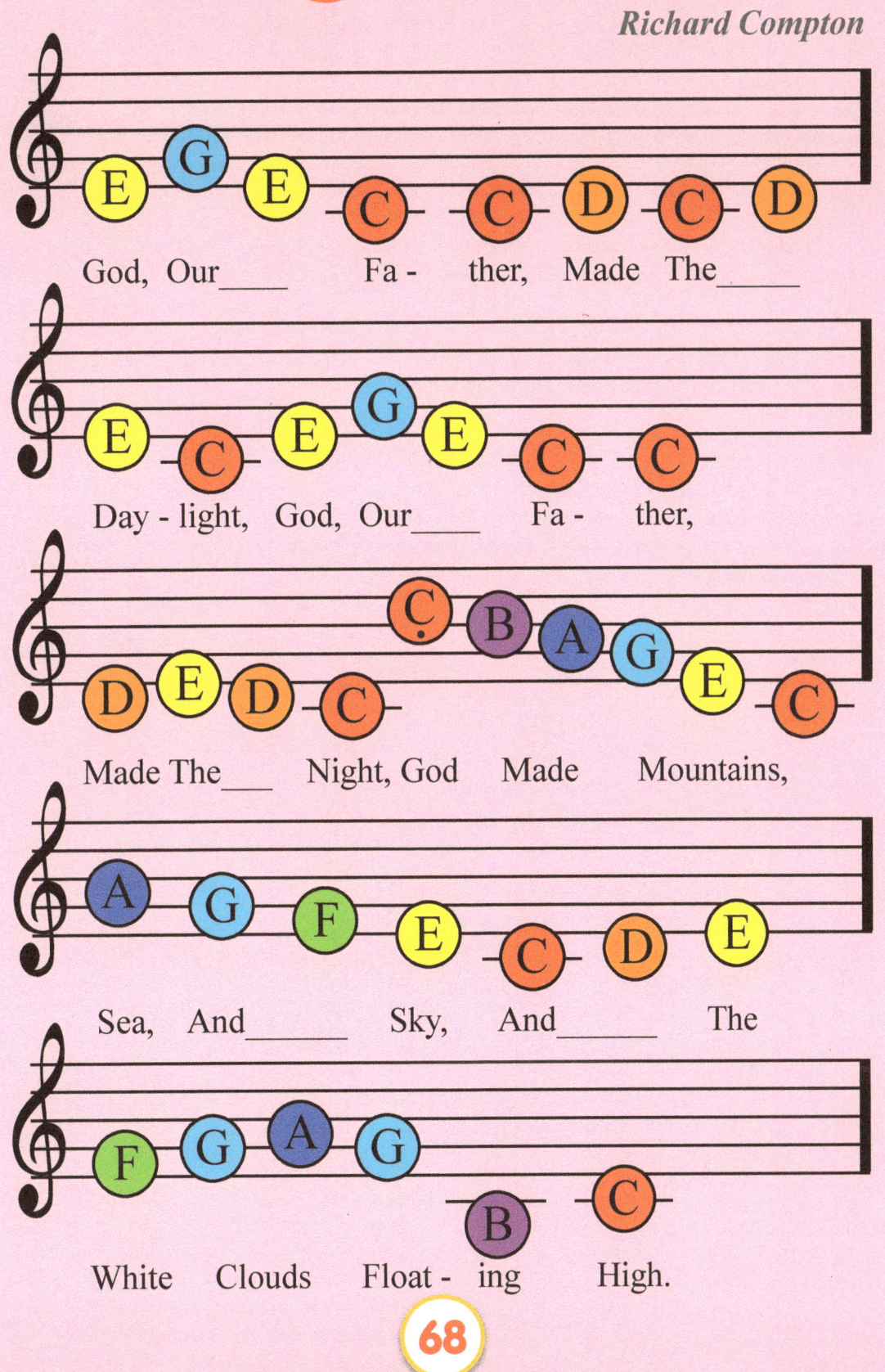

Richard Compton

E G E C C D C D
God, Our Fa - ther, Made The

E C E G E C C
Day - light, God, Our Fa - ther,

D E D C C B A G E C
Made The Night, God Made Mountains,

A G F E C D E
Sea, And Sky, And The

F G A G B C
White Clouds Float - ing High.

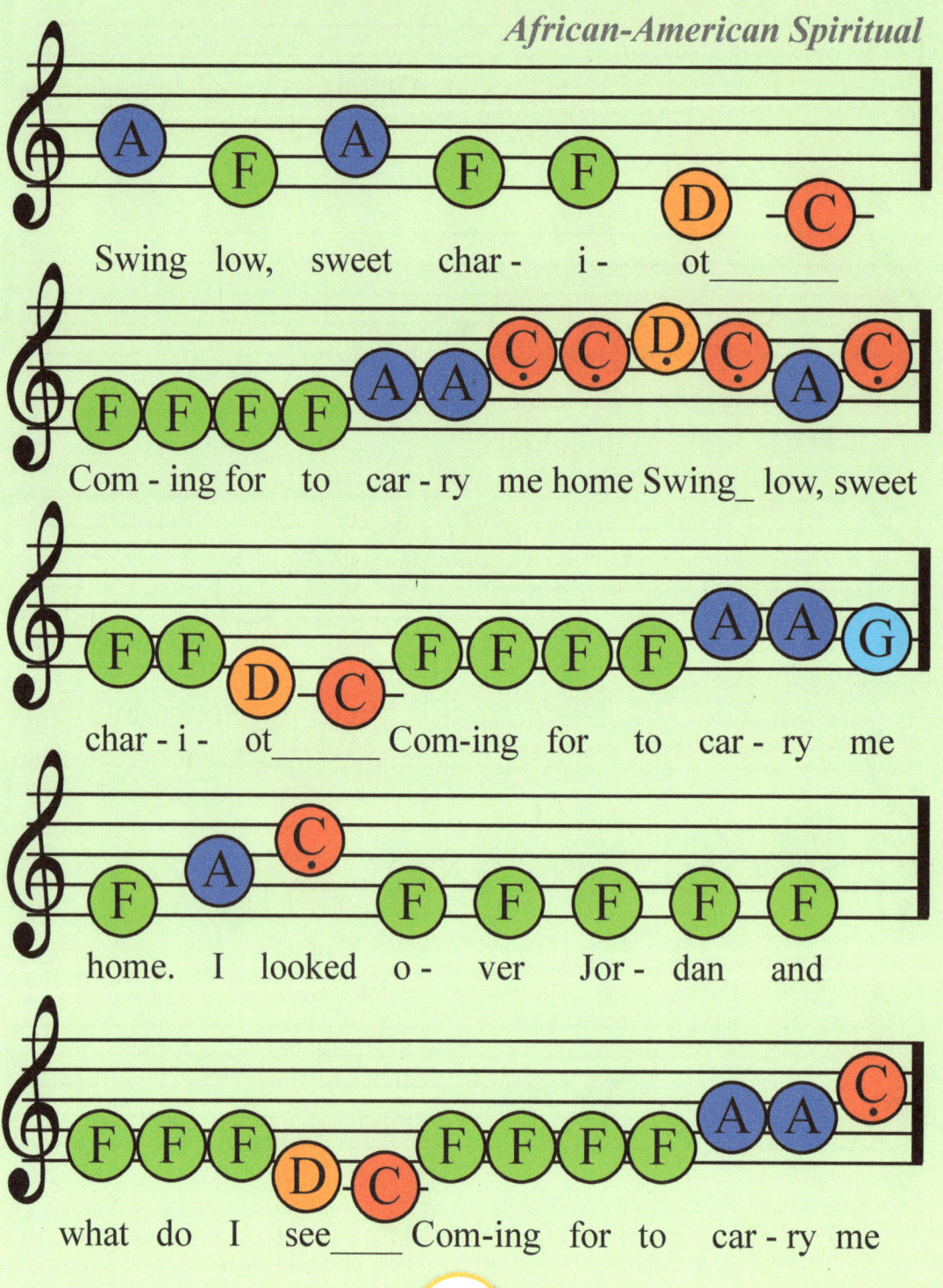

Swing Low, Sweet Chariot

African-American Spiritual

A F A F F D C
Swing low, sweet char - i - ot

F F F F A A C C D C A C
Com - ing for to car - ry me home Swing low, sweet

F F D C F F F F A A G
char - i - ot Com-ing for to car - ry me

F A C F F F F F
home. I looked o - ver Jor - dan and

F F F D C F F F F A A C
what do I see Com-ing for to car - ry me

69

home   A   band____   of   an - gels

com - ing   af - ter   me____

Com-ing   for   to   car - ry   me home Swing low, sweet

char - i - ot____ Com-ing   for   to   car - ry   me

home Swing____   low, sweet   char - i - ot____

Com - ing   for   to   car - ry   me   home

This Little Light of Mine

African-American Spiritual

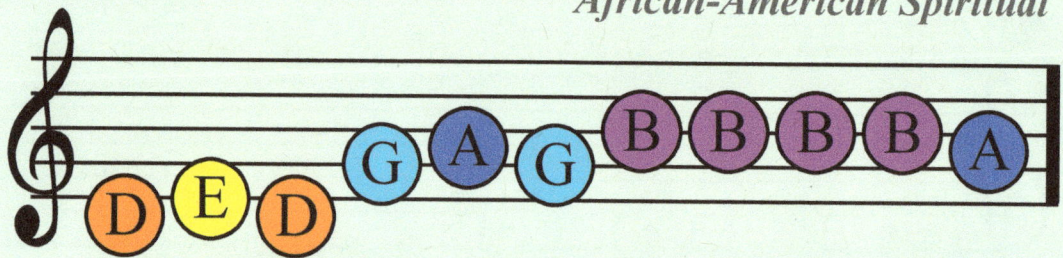

D E D G A G B B B B A
This lit-tle light of mine, I'm gon-na let it

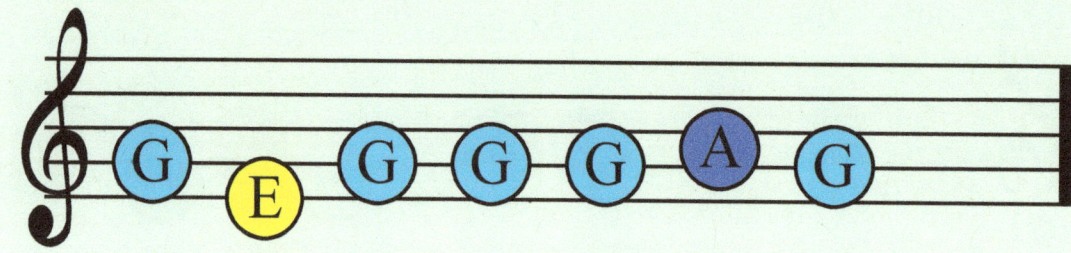

G E G G G A G
shine. This lit-tle light of mine,

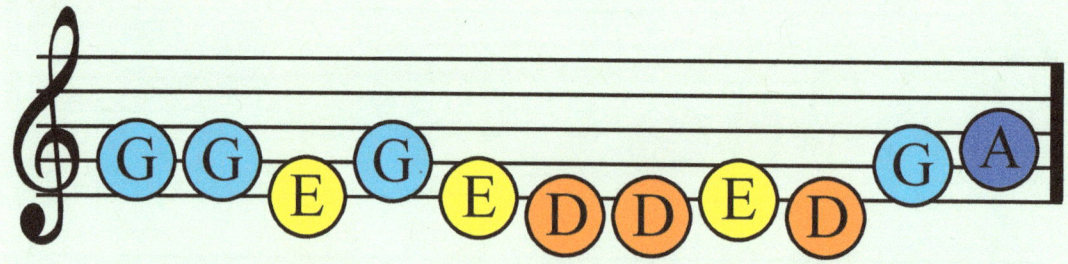

G G E G E D D E D G A
I'm gon-na let it shine. This lit-tle light of

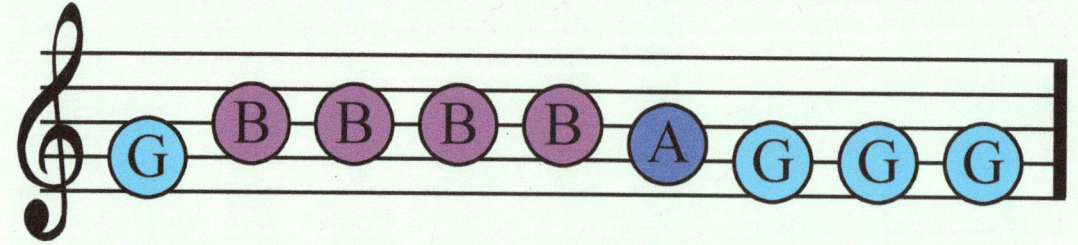

G B B B B A G G G
mine, I'm gon-na let it shine. Let it

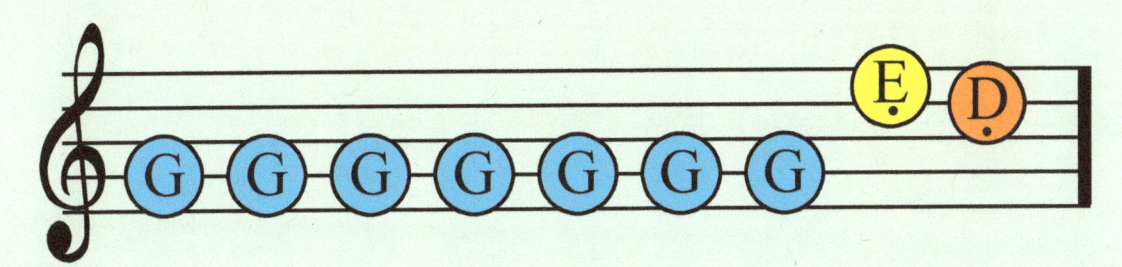

shine, let it shine, let it shine. Everywhere

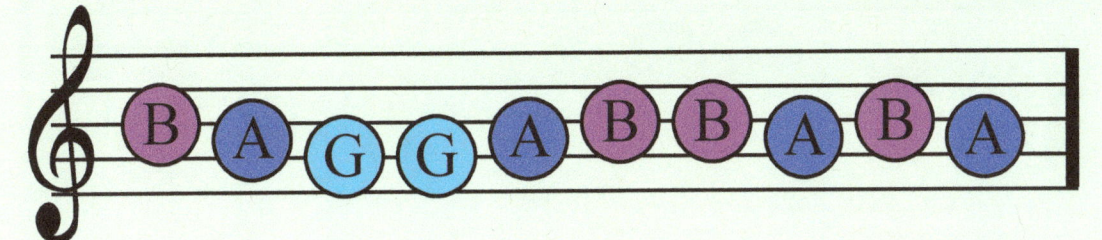

I go, I'm gon-na let it shine. Everywhere

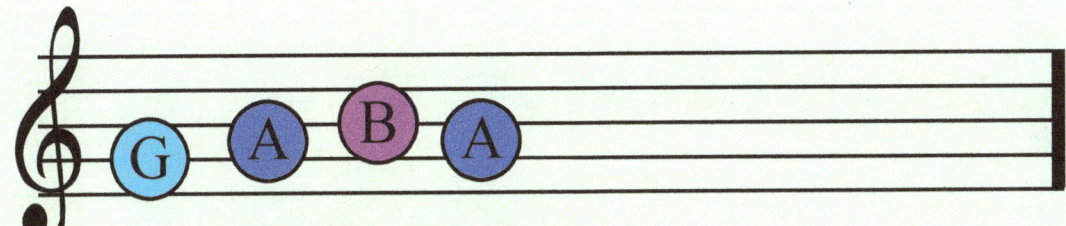

I go, I'm gonna let it shine.

Everywhere I go, I'm gonna let it shine.
Let it shine, let it shine, let it shine.
This little light of mine, I'm gonna let it shine.
This little light of mine, I'm gonna let it shine.
This little light of mine, I'm gonna let it shine.
Let it shine, let it shine, let it shine.
We will sing in peace,
We will sing in harmony.
We will sing in peace,
We will sing in harmony.
We will sing in peace,
We will sing in harmony.

There's a Meeting Here Tonight

African-American Spiritual

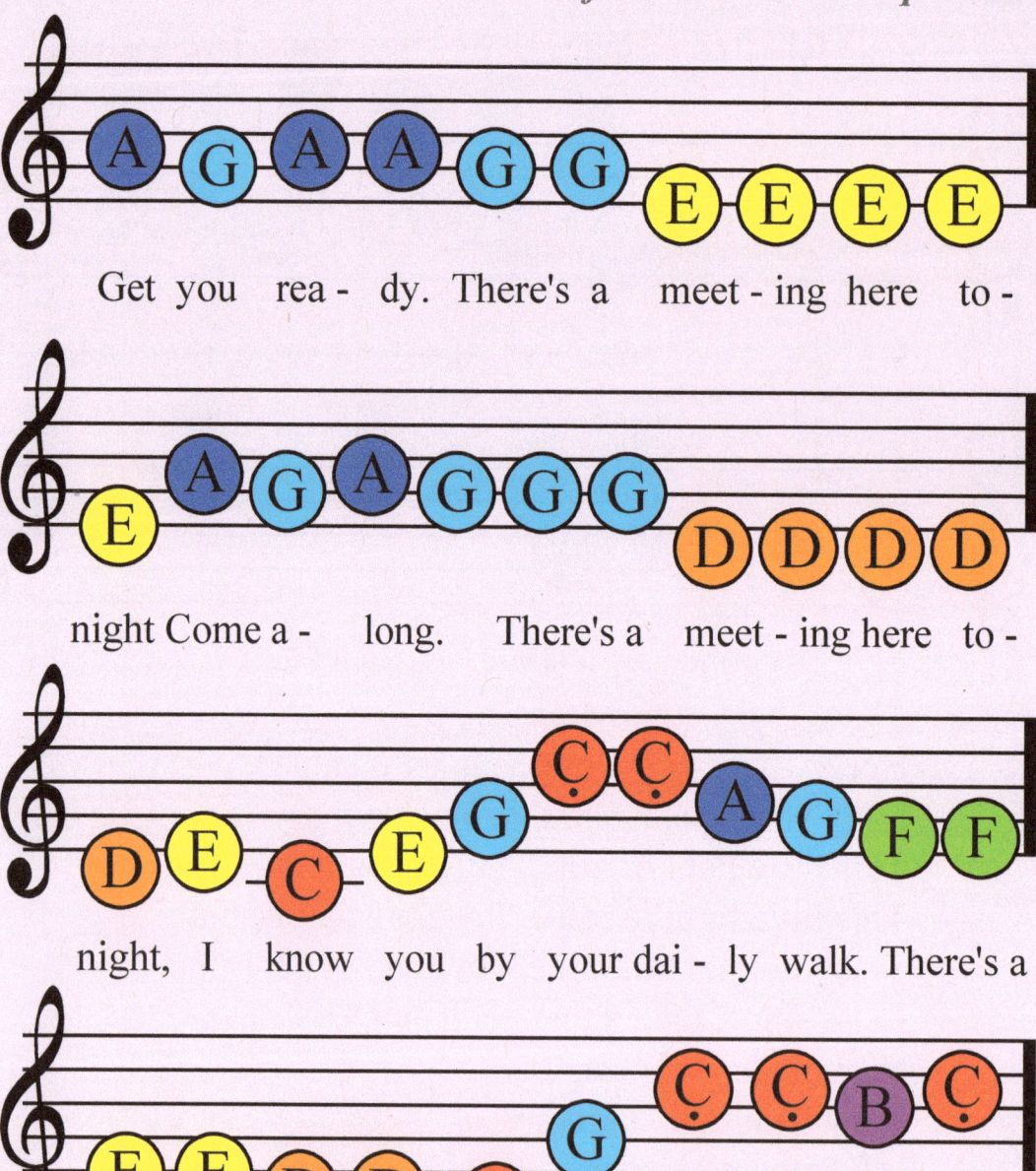

A G A A G G E E E E
Get you rea - dy. There's a meet - ing here to -

E A G A G G G D D D D
night Come a - long. There's a meet - ing here to -

D E C E G C C A G F F
night, I know you by your dai - ly walk. There's a

E E D D C G C C B C
meet - ing here to - night. Camp meet - ing down in the

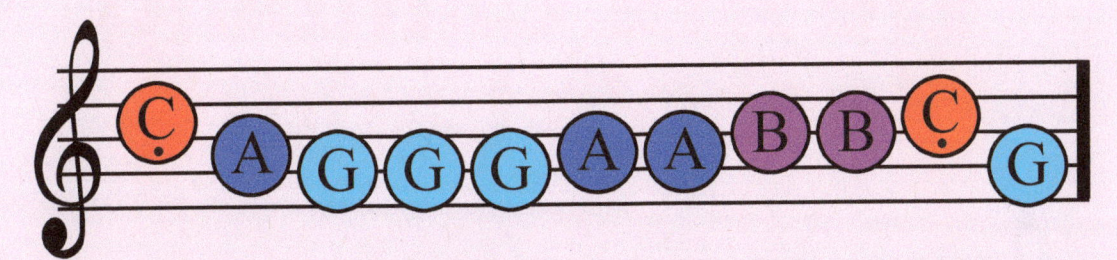

wil - der - ness, There's a meet - ing here to - night, I

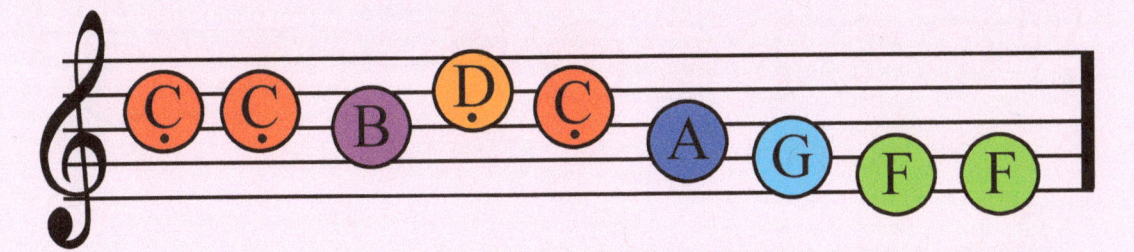

know it's a - mong the Me - tho - dists. There's a

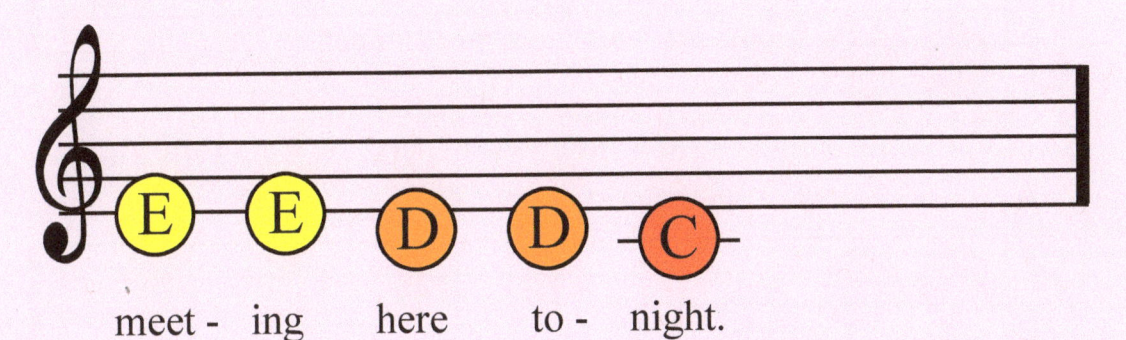

meet - ing here to - night.

Get you ready.
There's a meeting here tonight,
Come along.
There's a meeting here tonight.
I know you by your daily walk,
There's a meeting here tonight.

Get you ready,
There's a meeting here tonight.
Come along,
There's a meeting here tonight.
I know you by your daily walk,
There's a meeting here tonight.

You say you're aiming for the skies,
There's a meeting here tonight.
Why don't you stop your telling lies?
There's a meeting here tonight.

We Are Climbing Jacob's Ladder

African-American Spiritual

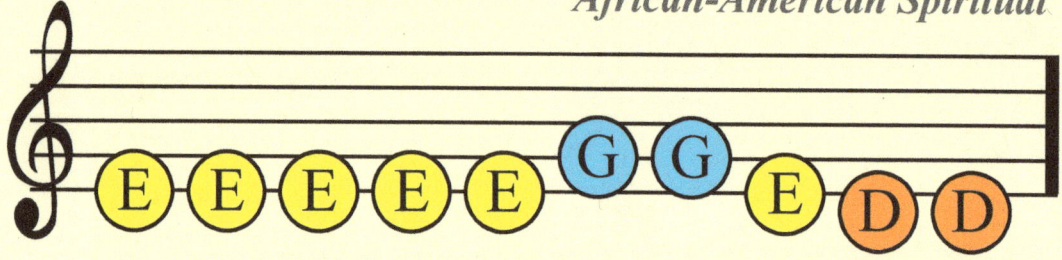

E E E E E G G E D D
We are climb - ing Ja - cob's lad - der, We are

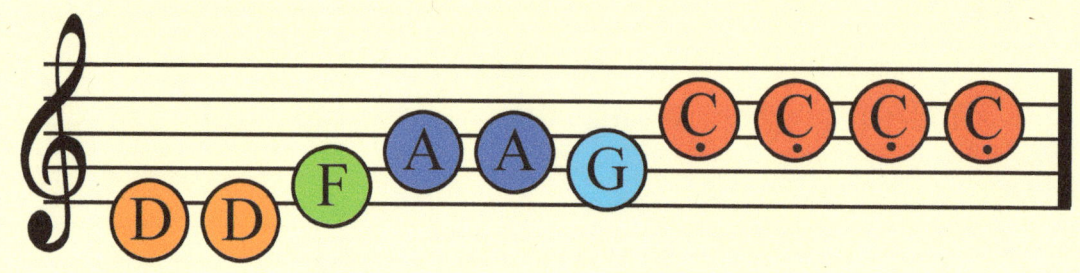

D D F A A G C C C C
climb - ing Ja - cob's lad - der, We are climbing

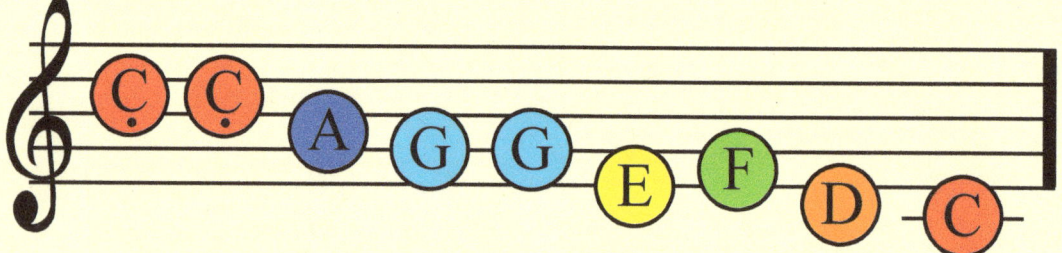

C C A G G E F D C
Ja - cob's lad - der, Sol - diers of the cross.

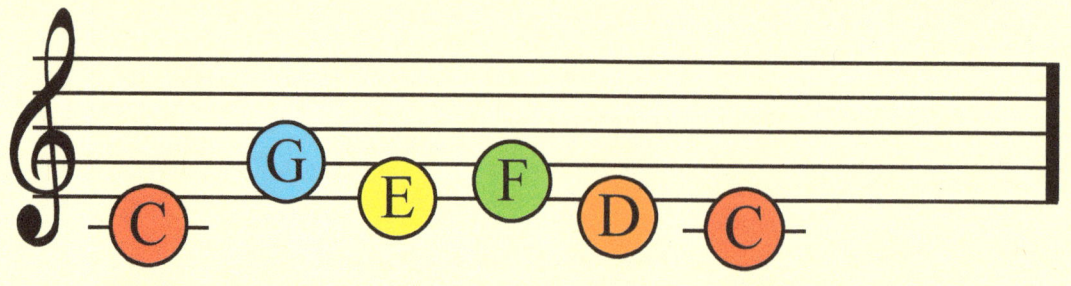

C G E F D C
cross. Sol - diers of the cross.

75

We Are Marching (Siyahamba)

South-African Hymn

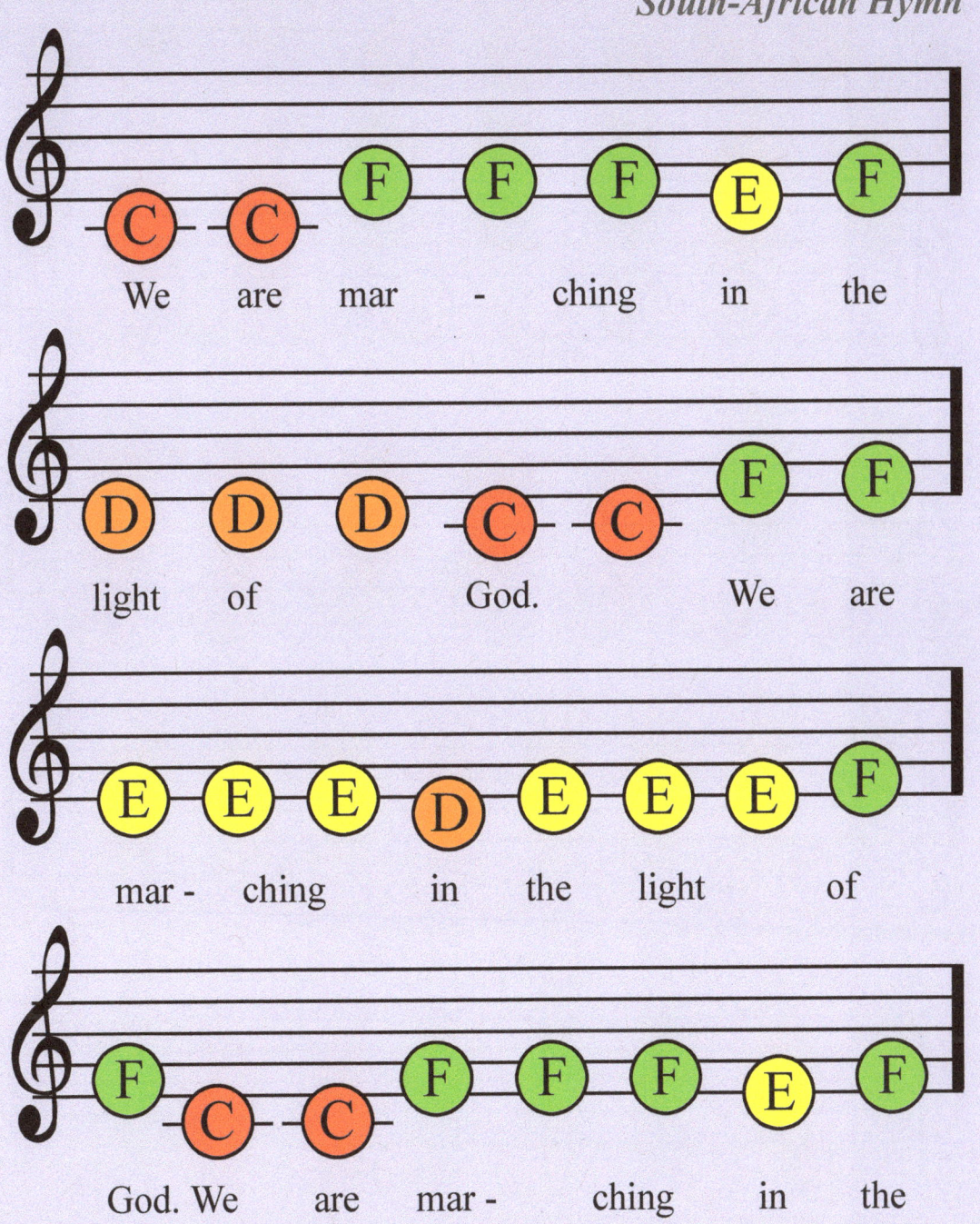

C C F F F E F
We are mar - ching in the

D D D C C F F
light of God. We are

E E E D E E E F
mar - ching in the light of

F C C F F F E F
God. We are mar - ching in the

light   of   God.   We   are

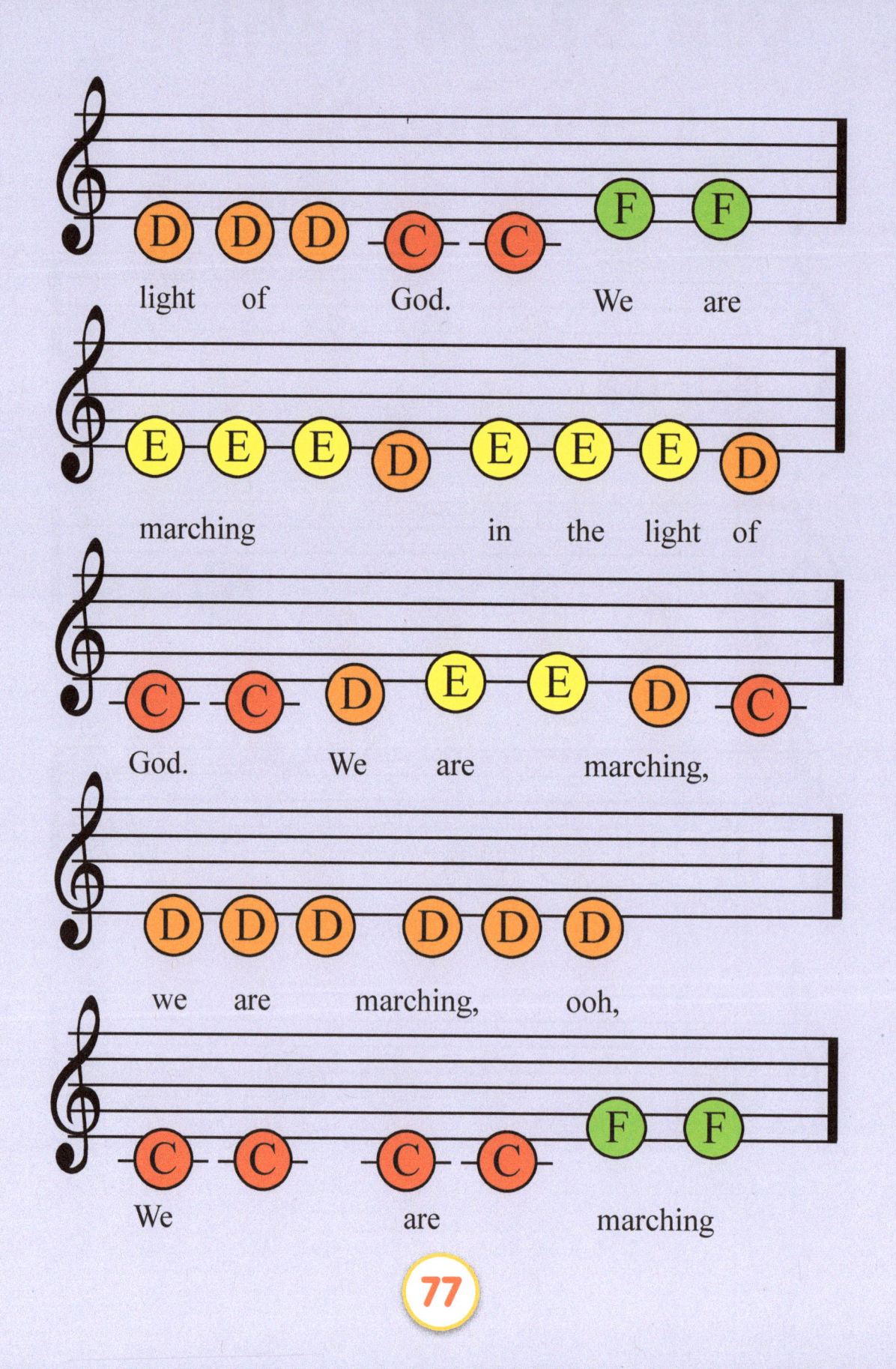

marching   in   the   light   of

God.   We   are   marching,

we   are   marching,   ooh,

We   are   marching

E E E D E E E D
in the light of God.

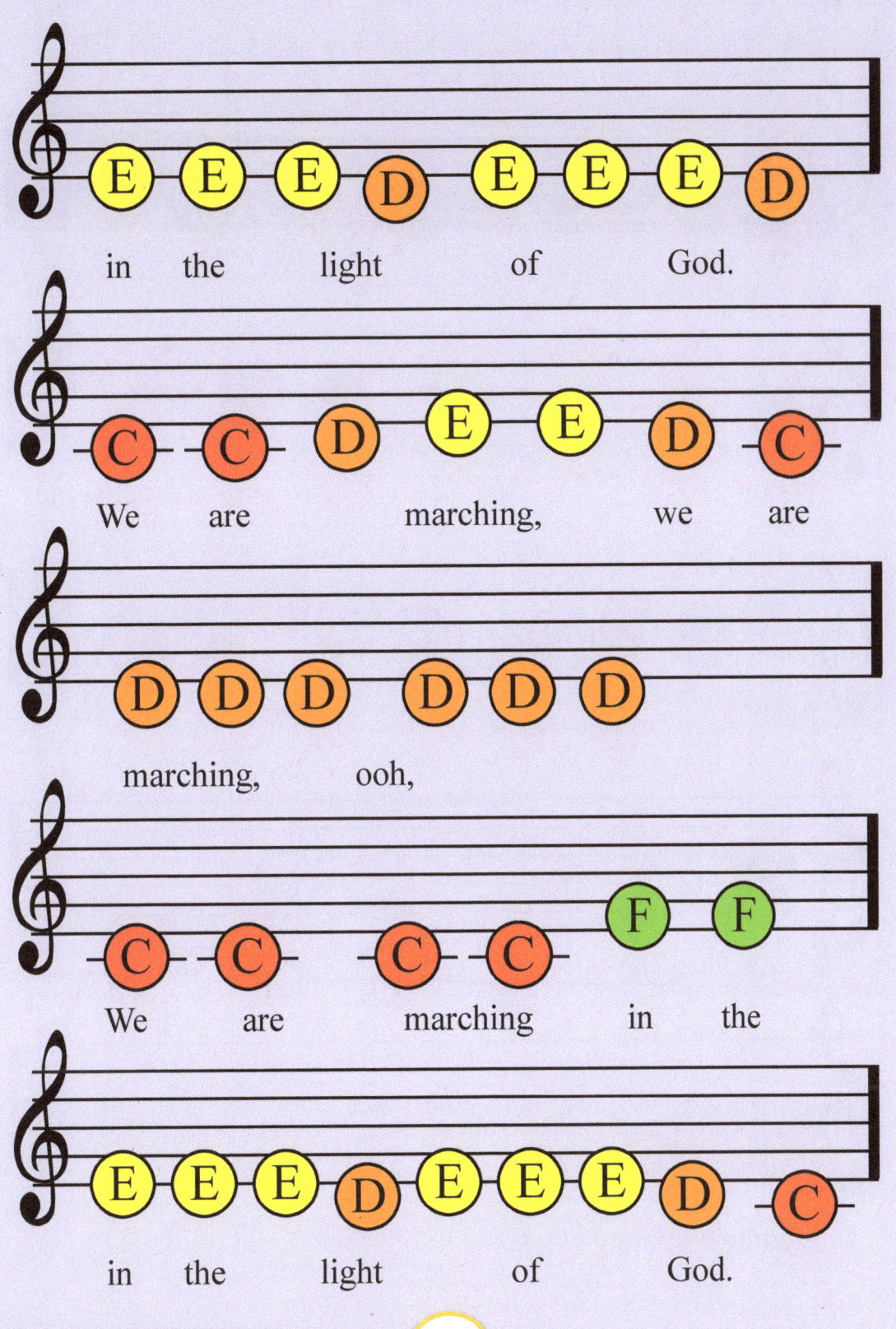

C C D E E D C
We are marching, we are

D D D D D D
marching, ooh,

C C C C F F
We are marching in the

E E E D E E E D C
in the light of God.

We Shall Overcome

Charles Albert Tindley

G G A A G F E G G A A
We shall o - ver-come___ We shall o - ver

G F E G G A B C D
come___ We shall o - ver - come, some

B A B A G A B C B A G
day___ Oh,___ deep in my heart

A G F E G G C F
I do be - lieve We shall o - ver

E D C
come some - day.

When the Saints Go Marchin' In

African-American Spiritual

Oh, when the saints go marchin' in, oh, when the
(C E F G   C E F G   C E F)

saints go marchin' in, I want to
(G   E   C   E   D   E   E   D)

be in that num-ber, oh, when the
(C   E   G   G   F   F   E   F)

saints go marchin' in.
(G   E   C   D   C   C)

Who Built the Ark?

African-American Spiritual

G G E D B A B A
Who built the ark? Noah, Noah

G G E D C C B B A A G
Who built the ark? Father Noah built the ark.

G G E D B A B A
Who built the ark? Noah, Noah

G G E D C C B B A A G
Who built the ark? Father Noah built the ark.

Old man Noah built the ark,___ he
built it out of__ a hick - o - ry bark.___
Built it long and wide and tall,___ with
plenty of room for the large and the small.__

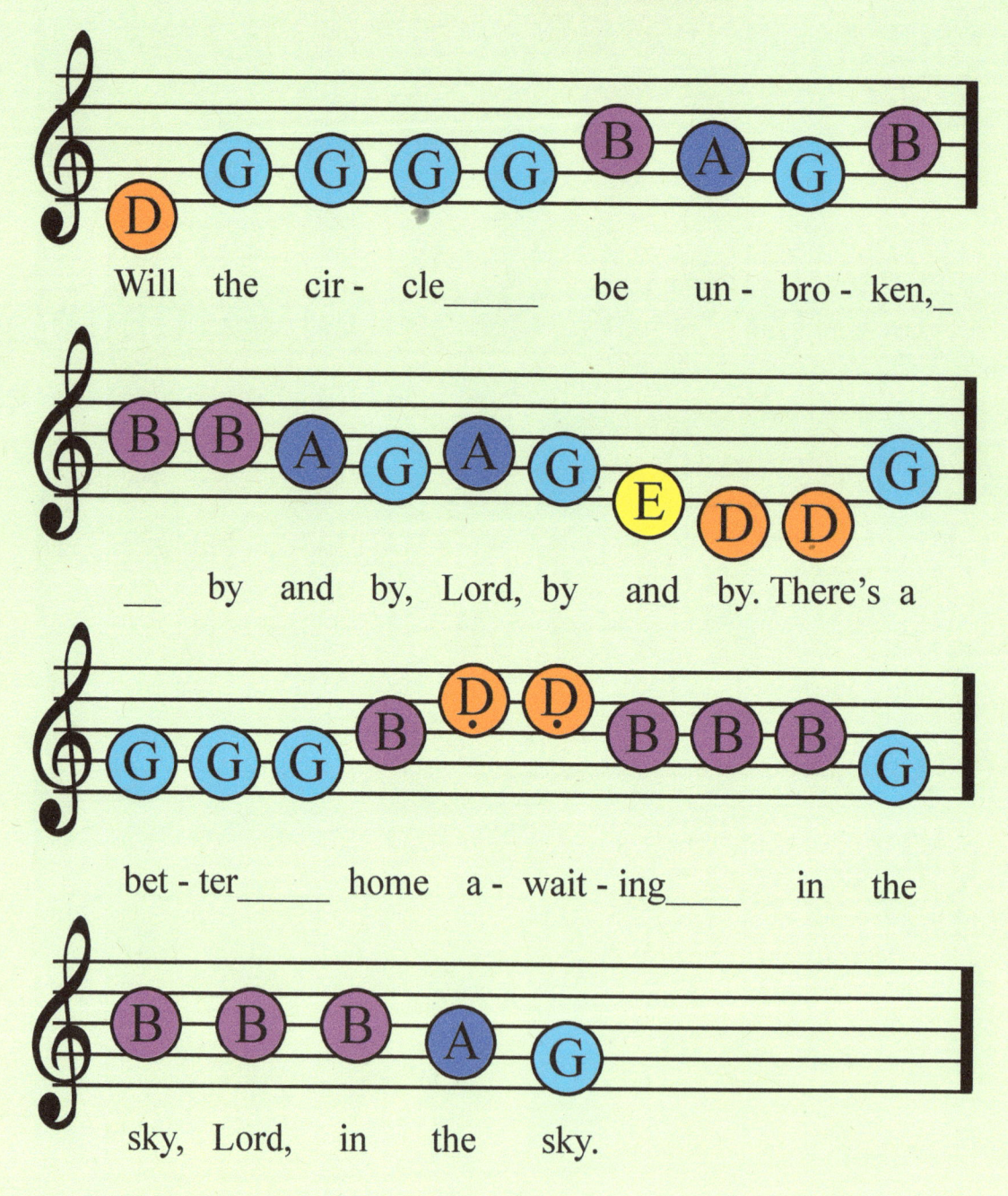

Will the Circle Be Unbroken

D G G G G B A G B
Will the cir - cle____ be un - bro - ken,_

B B A G A G E D D G
__ by and by, Lord, by and by. There's a

G G G B D D B B B G
bet - ter____ home a - wait - ing____ in the

B B B A G
sky, Lord, in the sky.

83